WRAP COOKBOOK NEW EDITION

Discover Sandwich Alternatives with Simple, Step-by-Step Recipes for Rolls, Wraps, and Foldovers—Perfect for Healthy Weight Loss and Everyday Enjoyment

HADLEY F. GREEN

Copyright © 2024 By HADLEY F. GREEN. All rights reserved worldwide.

No part of this book may be reproduced or transmitted in any form or by any means, electronic or mechanical, including photocopying, recording, or by any information storage and retrieval system, without written permission from the publisher, except for including brief quotations in a review.

Warning Disclaimer:

The purpose of this book is to educate and entertain. The author or publisher does not guarantee that anyone following the techniques, suggestions, tips, ideas, or strategies will become successful. The author and publisher shall have neither liability nor responsibility to anyone concerning any loss or damage caused, or alleged to be caused, directly or indirectly, by the information contained in this book.

This copyright notice and disclaimer apply to the entirety of the book and its contents, whether in print or electronic form and extend to all future editions or revisions of the book. Unauthorised use or reproduction of this book or its contents is strictly prohibited and may result in legal action.

TABLE OF CONTENTS

INTRODUCTION..................................7

    The Wrap Revolution 12

    Essential Equipment 15

    Understanding Wraps 17

    Meal Planning and Prep 22

CHAPTER 1: BREAKFAST WRAPS........ 25

    Classic English Breakfast Wrap ... 25

    Smoked Salmon and Cream Cheese Wrap 25

    Veggie-Packed Omelette Wrap..... 26

    Peanut Butter and Banana Breakfast Roll 27

    Full English Breakfast Burrito........ 27

    Greek Yogurt and Berry Breakfast Wrap 28

    Mushroom and Spinach Breakfast Quesadilla 28

    Ham and Cheese Breakfast Wrap..29

    Avocado Toast Wrap 29

    Scrambled Tofu Breakfast Wrap .. 30

    Nutella and Strawberry Crepe Wrap 30

    Bacon, Egg, and Cheese Wrap 31

    Apple and Cinnamon Breakfast Burrito.. 32

CHAPTER 2: LUNCH BOX HEROES 33

    Classic Chicken Caesar Wrap........ 33

    Tuna Salad Wrap............................. 33

    Mediterranean Hummus and Falafel Wrap.. 34

    Turkey and Cranberry Wrap 34

    Egg Mayonnaise and Cress Wrap.. 35

    BLT (Bacon, Lettuce, Tomato) Wrap 35

    Coronation Chicken Wrap 36

    Ploughman's Lunch Wrap 36

    Prawn and Avocado Wrap............. 37

    Roast Beef and Horseradish Wrap 37

Greek Salad Wrap 38

Pesto Chicken and Mozzarella Wrap
.... 39

Curried Egg Salad Wrap 40

CHAPTER 3: DINNER DELIGHTS 41

Spicy Beef and Bean Burrito 41

Crispy Duck Pancakes 41

Fish and Chips Wrap 42

Lamb Kofta Wrap with Tzatziki 43

Vegetable Stir-Fry Lettuce Wraps 43

BBQ Pulled Pork Wrap 44

Chicken Tikka Masala Wrap 45

Fajita-Style Steak Wrap 45

Spinach and Ricotta Cannelloni Wrap
.... 46

Teriyaki Tofu Wrap 46

Sausage and Mash Wrap 47

Vegetarian Chilli Wrap 47

Moroccan Lamb Wrap 48

CHAPTER 4: VEGETARIAN AND VEGAN DELIGHTS 49

Falafel and Hummus Wrap 49

Grilled Halloumi and Roasted Vegetable Wrap 49

Vegan 'Chicken' Caesar Wrap 50

Spicy Bean and Guacamole Burrito 51

Roasted Butternut Squash and Sage Wrap 51

Vegan 'Egg' Mayo Wrap 52

Mushroom Shawarma Wrap 52

Chickpea 'Tuna' Salad Wrap 53

Greek-Style Veggie Wrap 53

Tofu Scramble Breakfast Wrap 54

Lentil and Spinach Curry Wrap 54

Caprese Wrap with Balsamic Glaze
.... 55

Vegan 'Fish' Finger Wrap 56

CHAPTER 5: GLOBAL FLAVOURS 57

Mexican Street Corn Wrap 57

Japanese Teriyaki Chicken Wrap. 57

Indian Butter Chicken Wrap 58

Vietnamese Banh Mi Wrap 58

Greek Gyros Wrap 59

Korean BBQ Beef Wrap 59

Italian Caprese Wrap 60

Thai Green Curry Wrap 60

American Philly Cheesesteak Wrap 61

Middle Eastern Shawarma Wrap.... 61

Spanish Tortilla Wrap 62

Russian Beef Stroganoff Wrap 63

Jamaican Jerk Chicken Wrap 64

CHAPTER 6: HEALTHY AND LIGHT 65

Quinoa and Roasted Vegetable Wrap 65

Grilled Chicken and Avocado Lettuce Wrap 65

Smoked Salmon and Cucumber Roll 66

Turkey and Hummus Pinwheels 67

Tabbouleh and Feta Wrap.............. 67

Tofu and Vegetable Spring Rolls .. 68

Egg White and Spinach Breakfast Wrap 68

Lentil and Sweet Potato Wrap 69

Tuna Nicoise Salad Wrap 69

Cauliflower Rice and Black Bean Burrito 70

Grilled Prawn and Mango Wrap 70

Zucchini Noodle and Pesto Wrap ... 71

Beetroot Hummus and Goat Cheese Wrap 72

CHAPTER 7: PARTY AND PICNIC WRAPS 73

Mini Wrap Pinwheels Platter 73

Club Sandwich Wrap 73

Antipasti Wrap Skewers 74

Chicken and Stuffing Wrap Rolls .. 74

Smoked Salmon and Cream Cheese Spirals 75

Vegetable Crudité Hummus Wraps 75

Coronation Chicken Vol-au-Wrap . 76

Pesto and Sun-Dried Tomato Pinwheels.. 76

Ham and Cheese Wrap Straws....... 77

Egg and Watercress Finger Wraps 77

Roast Beef and Horseradish Spirals 78

Vegan Rainbow Veggie Wrap Bites 79

Prawn Cocktail Lettuce Cups 80

CHAPTER 8: SWEET TREATS AND DESSERT WRAPS 81

Banana and Nutella Crepe 81

Apple Pie Wrap 81

Strawberries and Cream Wrap 82

S'mores Wrap 82

Peanut Butter and Jelly Roll-Up.... 83

Blueberry Cheesecake Wrap 83

Cinnamon Sugar Churro Wrap 84

Lemon Meringue Wrap 84

Chocolate and Marshmallow Wrap 85

Peaches and Cream Wrap 85

Banoffee Pie Wrap 85

Berry Yogurt Parfait Wrap 86

Tropical Fruit Salad Wrap............. 86

CHAPTER 9: SAUCES, SPREADS, AND DIPS 87

Classic Hummus............................ 87

Tzatziki Sauce................................ 87

Guacamole 88

Salsa Fresca 88

Garlic Aioli..................................... 89

Tahini Sauce 89

Pesto 90

Chipotle Mayo................................ 90

Mango Chutney.............................. 91

BBQ Sauce 91

Sweet Chilli Sauce......................... 92

Herby Yogurt Dip 93

Baba Ganoush 94

CHAPTER 10: SIDE DISHES AND ACCOMPANIMENTS........................ 95

Crispy Sweet Potato Fries............. 95

Greek Salad................................... 95

Coleslaw.. 96

Tabbouleh 96

Potato Wedges.............................. 97

Corn on the Cob............................ 97

Garlic Green Beans 98

Roasted Mediterranean Vegetables 98

Quinoa Salad 99

Pickled Onions 99

Cajun Rice 100

Cucumber and Mint Raita 100

Spicy Kimchi 101

Measurement Conversions 102

MEAL PLAN TIMETABLE ACCORDING TO NUTRITION.. 103

INTRODUCTION

MY WRAP JOURNEY: HOW I FELL IN LOVE WITH WRAP COOKING

I remember the day I fell head over heels for wrap cooking as if it were yesterday. It was a dreary Tuesday afternoon in Manchester, and I was a frazzled uni student with a fridge full of odds and ends but no idea what to cook for tea. As I stared blankly into the refrigerator, my eyes landed on a pack of tortillas I'd bought on a whim. Little did I know, those humble flatbreads were about to change my culinary life forever.

With a shrug, I decided to give it a go. I warmed up a tortilla, spread some leftover hummus on it, and tossed in whatever veggies I could find - some wilted spinach, a slightly wrinkly tomato, and the last bits of cucumber. A drizzle of olive oil, a sprinkle of salt and pepper, and voila! I rolled it up (rather messily, I must admit) and took a bite. The explosion of flavours and textures was a revelation. The warm, soft tortilla embraced the cool, creamy hummus. The vegetables added freshness and crunch. It was a perfect balance of comforting and refreshing, hearty yet light. At that moment, I realised I'd stumbled upon something brilliant.

From that day forward, I was on a mission. I experimented with every type of wrap I could get my hands on - flour tortillas, corn tortillas, lettuce leaves, rice paper, nori sheets - you name it, I tried to wrap something in it. I filled them with traditional British fare like bangers and mash, gave them an Indian twist with chicken tikka and raita, and even turned my gran's Sunday roast into a portable feast. As I delved deeper into the world of wraps, I discovered their incredible versatility. They were perfect for using up leftovers, ideal for packed lunches, and brilliant for feeding a crowd. Whether I was rushing to lectures, hosting impromptu dinner parties, or trying to impress a date, wraps always came to my rescue.

But it wasn't just about convenience. As I honed my wrap-making skills, I found myself becoming more adventurous in the kitchen. I started experimenting with flavour combinations I'd never have considered before. I learned about balancing textures and temperatures. I even picked up some nifty knife skills trying to julienne vegetables for the perfect crunch. Wrap cooking also opened my eyes to global cuisines. From Mexican burritos to Middle Eastern shawarmas, from Vietnamese summer rolls to Japanese hand rolls - the world seemed to have a wrap for every occasion. Each culture had its techniques, flavours, and traditions surrounding wrapped foods, and exploring these became my passion.

As my love for wrap cooking grew, so did my circle of friends. There's something inherently social about wrap meals - perhaps it's the informality, the hands-on nature of the eating, or simply the fun of creating your perfect combination. Whatever the reason, I found myself hosting more gatherings, sharing my creations, and bonding over our mutual love for these versatile meals.

Over the years, wrap cooking has been my constant companion. It saw me through uni, helped me impress at potlucks, saved countless weeknight dinners, and even played a starring role at my wedding (yes, we had a build-your-own-wrap station, and it was a hit!). Now, as I sit here writing this cookbook, I'm filled with excitement at the thought of sharing my wrap journey with you. Whether you're a complete novice in the kitchen or a seasoned cook looking for fresh ideas, I hope this book will inspire you to embrace the wonderful world of wraps. So, let's embark on this delicious adventure together, shall we?

THE ART AND JOY OF WRAP-MAKING

When I first started my wrap-making journey, I thought it was all about slapping some ingredients onto a flatbread and rolling it up. Oh, how wrong I was! As I delved deeper into this culinary art form (because yes, I firmly believe wrap-making is an art), I discovered a world of nuance, technique, and creativity that continues to fascinate me to this day. At its core, the art of wrap-making is about harmony. It's about bringing together a variety of flavours, textures, and even temperatures in a way that creates a perfect bite every time. Think about it - a great wrap isn't just tasty; it's an experience. The soft chew of the wrap itself, the burst of flavour from the filling, the crunch of fresh vegetables, the zing of a well-matched sauce - when all these elements come together, it's nothing short of culinary magic.

But achieving this harmony isn't always straightforward. It takes practice, experimentation, and a willingness to think outside the box. Over the years, I've learned some key principles that I believe form the foundation of great wrap-making:

1. Balance is key: A good wrap needs a balance of flavours (salty, sweet, sour, umami), textures (soft, crunchy, creamy), and temperatures (warm and cool elements).

2. Don't overstuff: It's tempting to pile on the fillings, but an overstuffed wrap is hard to eat and often falls apart. Less is often more.

3. Layer strategically: The order in which you add ingredients can make a big difference. For instance, putting cheese next to a warm protein helps it melt slightly.

4. Master the roll: A well-rolled wrap stays together and ensures you get a bit of everything in each bite. It's a skill worth perfecting.

5. Experiment fearlessly: Some of my best creations have come from unexpected combinations. Don't be afraid to try new things!

The joy of wrap-making, for me, comes from the endless possibilities. With a simple change of wrap or a swap of sauce, you can transform a familiar combination into something entirely new. It's a form of cooking that encourages creativity and playfulness.

I love the way wrap-making connects us to global culinary traditions. From the Mexican burrito to the Middle Eastern shawarma, from the Vietnamese summer roll to the Japanese temaki, cultures around the world have their own unique wrapped dishes. Exploring these traditions has not only expanded my culinary repertoire but has also given me a deeper appreciation for the rich tapestry of global cuisine. There's also a wonderful social aspect to wrap cooking. Whether it's a casual weeknight dinner with family or a big gathering with friends, laying out a spread of wraps and fillings and letting everyone create their perfect combination always leads to a fun, interactive meal. It's a great way to cater to different dietary needs and preferences too - everyone can customise their wrap to their liking.

One of the most joyful aspects of wrap-making for me is its accessibility. You don't need fancy equipment or professional training to make a delicious wrap. With some basic ingredients and a little creativity, anyone can create something tasty. It's a form of cooking that's open to everyone, from complete beginners to seasoned chefs. As you embark on your wrap-making journey, I encourage you to embrace both the art and the joy of it. Don't worry too much about getting everything perfect right away. Allow yourself to experiment, make mistakes, and discover your favourite combinations.

Remember, every great wrap starts with a single fold. So roll up your sleeves, gather your ingredients, and let's dive into the wonderful world of wraps together. I promise you, it's a journey filled with delicious discoveries, creative breakthroughs, and plenty of joy.

HOW THIS BOOK WILL TRANSFORM YOU INTO A WRAP MASTER

Welcome to "Wrap Cookbook: New Edition"! If you're holding this book, you're already on your way to becoming a wrap master. Whether you're a complete novice in the kitchen or a seasoned cook looking to expand your repertoire, this book is designed to take your wrap-making skills to the next level. Let me give you a taste of what's in store and how this book will transform your culinary journey.

First things first, let's talk about the structure of this book. I've carefully crafted it to take you from wrap novice to wrap virtuoso in a logical, easy-to-follow progression. Here's what you can expect:

1. Foundations of Wrap Mastery: We'll start with the basics. You'll learn about different types of wraps, essential equipment, and key ingredients to stock in your pantry. We'll cover fundamental techniques like choosing the right wrap for your filling, mastering the perfect fold, and balancing flavours and textures.

2. Recipe Chapters: The heart of this book is, of course, the recipes. Each chapter focuses on a different category of wraps, from breakfast wraps to start your day right, to party wraps that will make you the star of any gathering. Every recipe is designed to be easy to follow, with clear instructions and helpful tips.

3. Beyond the Basics: As you progress, you'll find sections dedicated to more advanced techniques, global wrap traditions, and creative fusion ideas. These will help you take your wrap game to the next level.

4. Troubleshooting and Tips: Throughout the book, you'll find boxes with common pitfalls and how to avoid them, as well as pro tips to elevate your wrap-making.

5. Dietary Considerations: I've included chapters and recipes catering to various dietary needs, including vegetarian, vegan, gluten-free, and low-carb options.

NOW, LET'S TALK ABOUT HOW THIS BOOK WILL TRANSFORM YOU INTO A WRAP MASTER:

Building Confidence: One of my main goals with this book is to build your confidence in the kitchen. We'll start with simple recipes and gradually introduce more complex techniques and flavour combinations. Before you know it, you'll be creating your signature wraps with flair.

Expanding Your Culinary Horizons: Through the diverse recipes in this book, you'll explore flavours and techniques from around the world. You'll learn how different cultures approach wrapped foods and how you can incorporate these ideas into your cooking.

Mastering Techniques: From the perfect fold to balancing flavours, you'll learn all the techniques you need to create stellar wraps. We'll break down each skill into easy-to-follow steps, with plenty of photos to guide you.

Encouraging Creativity: While the recipes in this book are delicious as they are, I've designed them to be springboards for your creativity. You'll learn the principles behind great wrap-making, enabling you to invent your unique combinations.

Practical Skills: The skills you'll learn go beyond just making wraps. You'll improve your knife skills, learn about flavour pairing, and develop a knack for creating balanced meals – all transferable skills that will benefit your overall cooking.

Lifestyle Integration: This book isn't just about recipes; it's about integrating wrap cooking into your lifestyle. You'll learn about meal planning, batch cooking, and how to use wraps to reduce food waste and save time in the kitchen.

Problem-Solving: Throughout the book, you'll find solutions to common wrap-making challenges. Soggy wraps? Fillings falling out? Uneven flavour distribution? We've got you covered.

Nutritional Knowledge: You'll gain an understanding of how to create nutritionally balanced wraps, making it easier to incorporate these versatile meals into a healthy diet.

By the time you reach the end of this book, you'll have a comprehensive understanding of wrap cooking. You'll be able to confidently create a wide variety of wraps, from quick weeknight dinners to impressive party spreads. You'll have the skills to improvise with whatever ingredients you have on hand, and the knowledge to balance flavours and textures like a pro.

But more than that, I hope this book will instil in you the same love and excitement for wrap cooking that I feel. I hope it will inspire you to experiment, to push boundaries, and to share your creations with others. Because at the end of the day, that's what being a wrap master is all about – not just making delicious food, but spreading joy through your culinary creations.

So, are you ready to begin your transformation? Let's turn the page and start our journey to wrap mastery together. Trust me, it's going to be a delicious adventure!

THE WRAP REVOLUTION

WHAT MAKES WRAPS SO BRILLIANT

In my years of cooking and eating, I've come across few foods as versatile and exciting as wraps. But what exactly makes them so brilliant? Let me break it down for you.

First off, wraps are the ultimate canvas for creativity. Think about it you've got this blank slate of a tortilla, flatbread, or leaf, and you can fill it with literally anything your heart desires. It's like having a mini food festival in every bite! I've made wraps with everything from traditional fillings like grilled chicken and salad to more adventurous combinations like roast beef with Yorkshire pudding bits (trust me, it works!). The possibilities are truly endless. Wraps are also incredibly practical. In our fast-paced world, we often need meals that can keep up with us and wraps fit the bill perfectly. They're portable, easy to eat on the go, and can be prepared in advance without losing their appeal. I can't count the number of times a well-packed wrap has saved me during a busy workday or a long journey.

Another brilliant aspect of wraps is their ability to transform leftovers. That bit of Sunday roast, the last spoonful of curry, or those lonely vegetables at the back of the fridge wrap them up, and suddenly you've got a whole new meal! It's like culinary magic, and it's saved me from food waste more times than I can count. Wraps are also fantastic for catering to different dietary needs. Whether you're cooking for a vegan friend, a gluten-free family member, or a picky eater, wraps can be easily adapted to suit anyone's preferences. You can switch up the wrap itself use a gluten-free tortilla, a large lettuce leaf, or even a sheet of nori and then customize the fillings to your heart's content.

Lastly, let's not forget the fun factor. There's something inherently enjoyable about assembling and eating a wrap. It's hands-on, it's customizable, and it brings a bit of playfulness to mealtime. Whether you're having a casual dinner with family or hosting a party, setting out a spread of wrap ingredients always leads to a good time. In essence, wraps are brilliant because they embody everything we love about food creativity, practicality, versatility, inclusivity, and fun. They're a true revolution in how we approach cooking and eating, and I'm thrilled to guide you through this exciting culinary landscape.

HEALTH BENEFITS OF WRAP-BASED MEALS

Now, I know what you might be thinking "Aren't wraps just sandwiches in disguise? How healthy can they be?" Well, let me tell you, wrap-based meals can be incredibly nutritious when done right. They offer some unique health benefits that might surprise you.

First and foremost, wraps give you perfect portion control. The size of your wrap naturally limits how much you can stuff into it (although I've certainly tried to test those limits!). This built-in portion control can be a great help if you're watching your intake or trying to maintain a balanced diet.

Wraps also offer an excellent opportunity to pack in the vegetables. I always aim for at least two or three different veggies in my wraps, which helps me reach my five-a-day without even trying. From crisp lettuce and juicy tomatoes to grilled peppers and sautéed spinach, the possibilities are endless. And because the veggies are wrapped up with other tasty ingredients, even veggie-sceptics often find themselves enjoying them more.

Another health benefit of wrap-based meals is their potential for balanced nutrition. A well-constructed wrap can easily incorporate all the major food groups you've got your carbs from the wrap itself, protein from fillings like chicken, fish, or beans, healthy fats from avocado or a drizzle of olive oil, and of course, plenty of vitamins and minerals from your vegetables. It's like a complete meal, all rolled up in one convenient package!

Wraps can also be a great option for those watching their calorie intake. By choosing a whole grain wrap and loading up on lean proteins and vegetables, you can create a filling meal that's relatively low in calories. I've found this particularly helpful when I'm trying to eat lighter I can still enjoy a satisfying, tasty meal without feeling like I'm depriving myself.

For those with specific dietary needs, wraps can be a godsend. Need to go gluten-free? There are plenty of gluten-free wrap options available, or you can use large lettuce leaves for a super low-carb option. Watching your sodium? You're in control of exactly what goes into your wrap, so you can easily keep the salt content in check. Vegetarian or vegan? Load up on grilled veggies, hummus, and plant-based proteins for a delicious and nutritious meal.

Lastly, let's talk about fibre. Many store-bought sandwiches and fast food options are in this department, but wraps give you the perfect opportunity to boost your fibre intake. Choose a whole grain wrap, add some beans or lentils, throw in a variety of vegetables, and you've got yourself a fibre-rich meal that'll keep you feeling full and satisfied.

Remember, though, that the health benefits of your wrap ultimately depend on what you put in it. While a wrap filled with fried foods and heavy sauces might be tasty, it won't offer the same nutritional benefits as one packed with lean proteins, whole grains, and plenty of veg. But that's the beauty of wraps you're in control, and you can make them as healthy as you like!

SUSTAINABILITY AND ECO-FRIENDLY ASPECTS OF WRAP COOKING

In today's world, we're all becoming more aware of the impact our food choices have on the environment. That's why I'm excited to share with you how wrap cooking can be a more sustainable and eco-friendly way to prepare meals.

First off, wrap cooking is brilliant for reducing food waste. We've all had those moments where we open the fridge to find a random assortment of leftovers and bits and bobs that don't seem to go together. In the past, I might have let these languish until they were past their best. But now? I see the makings of a delicious wrap! By using wraps as a base, you can combine small amounts of different ingredients to create a whole new meal. It's like a delicious form of recycling!

Wrap cooking also lends itself well to plant-based meals, which typically have a lower environmental impact than meat-heavy dishes. Now, I'm not saying you need to go full vegetarian (although if you want to, wraps are a great way to do it!). But even incorporating more plant-based wraps into your routine can make a difference. I've found that wraps are a fantastic way to experiment with vegetarian and vegan options things like grilled vegetables, hummus, falafel, or plant-based proteins can make for incredibly satisfying meals.

Another eco-friendly aspect of wrap cooking is its energy efficiency. Many wrap recipes require minimal cooking if any at all. This means less energy is used in food preparation compared to dishes that need long cooking times. And when you do need to cook components of your wrap, it's often quick a brief sauté or grill is usually all it takes. This not only saves energy but also keeps your kitchen cool in the summer months!

Wraps are also great for reducing packaging waste. Instead of buying pre-packaged sandwiches or ready meals, you can buy ingredients in bulk or with minimal packaging and assemble your wraps at home. I like to use reusable containers to store my wrap ingredients, cutting down even further on single-use plastics.

Let's talk about seasonal eating, too. Wrap recipes are easy to adapt to whatever produce is in season. In the summer, I love filling my wraps with fresh, local tomatoes and cucumbers. In the winter, I might use roasted root vegetables or sautéed greens. By eating seasonally, you're not only getting the best flavours, but you're also reducing the carbon footprint associated with out-of-season produce that's been shipped from far away.

Lastly, wrap cooking can be a great way to support local food systems. Because you're often using fresh ingredients, it's easy to incorporate produce from local farms or farmers' markets into your wraps. This not only supports your local economy but also reduces the distance your food travels to get to your plate.

Of course, the sustainability of your wrap cooking ultimately depends on the choices you make. Opting for locally sourced, seasonal ingredients, reducing meat consumption, and minimizing food waste are all steps in the right direction. But that's what I love about wrap cooking it gives you the flexibility to make choices that align with your values, all while enjoying delicious, satisfying meals.

As we move through this cookbook, keep these sustainable aspects in mind. You'll find that many of the recipes and techniques we'll explore naturally lend themselves to eco-friendly cooking. It's just another reason to love the wrap revolution!

ESSENTIAL EQUIPMENT

Before we dive into the delicious world of wrap-making, let's make sure you've got the right tools for the job. Don't worry, you won't need to break the bank or clutter your kitchen with loads of gadgets. You probably already have most of what you need!

MUST-HAVE TOOLS FOR YOUR WRAP KITCHEN

1. Cutting Board: A good, sturdy cutting board is essential. I prefer a large wooden one for most prep work, but having a separate plastic board for meats can be handy for food safety.

2. Sharp Knives: You'll need a chef's knife for chopping vegetables and meats, and a smaller paring knife for more delicate work. Keep them sharp - a sharp knife is safer and makes prep work a breeze.

3. Measuring Cups and Spoons: Precision can be the difference between a good wrap and a great one, especially when you're making sauces or dressings.

4. Mixing Bowls: A set of various sizes will serve you well. I use them for everything from tossing salads to marinating proteins.

5. Colander: Essential for washing vegetables and draining canned beans.

6. Grater: For cheese, vegetables, and even zesting citrus fruits. A box grater is versatile, but a Microplane can be great for finer work.

7. Frying Pan or Griddle: For warming wraps and cooking fillings. A non-stick surface can be helpful, but it's not essential.

8. Tongs: These are brilliant for handling hot wraps or turning ingredients as they cook.

9. Wooden Spoons and Spatulas: For stirring, mixing, and serving.

10. Airtight Containers: Crucial for storing prepped ingredients and leftovers.

NICE-TO-HAVE GADGETS TO UP YOUR WRAP GAME

While not essential, these items can make wrap-making even more enjoyable:

1. Food Processor: Brilliant for making homemade hummus, salsas, or quickly chopping vegetables.

2. Mandoline: For achieving uniformly thin slices of vegetables. Just mind your fingers!

3. Garlic Press: If you love garlic as much as I do, this can be a real time-saver.

4. Citrus Juicer: For easily adding fresh lemon or lime juice to your recipes.

5. Electric Grill or Panini Press: Great for making hot, pressed wraps.

6. Herb Scissors: These multi-bladed scissors make short work of chopping fresh herbs.

7. Avocado Slicer: A fun gadget if you're an avocado fanatic like me.

SETTING UP YOUR WRAP-MAKING STATION

Efficiency is key when making wraps, especially if you're preparing them for a crowd. Here's how I set up my wrap-making station:

1. Prep Area: This is where you'll chop vegetables, cook proteins, and prepare other fillings. Keep your cutting board, knives, and prep bowls here.

2. Assembly Line: Set this up with your wraps, fillings, and sauces arranged in the order you'll use them. I like to put the wrap down first, then proteins, vegetables, cheese, and finally sauces or dressings.

3. Cooking Station: If you're making hot wraps, set up your pan or grill next to your assembly line for easy transfer.

4. Serving Area: Have plates or paper wraps ready for your finished creations.

5. Clean-Up Station: Keep a damp cloth or paper towels handy for quick clean-ups.

Remember, the key is to organize your space in a way that feels natural and efficient for you. As you make more wraps, you'll develop your perfect system!

UNDERSTANDING WRAPS

Now that we've got our equipment sorted, let's talk about the star of the show – the wraps themselves. Understanding the different types of wraps and how to use them is key to creating delicious, well-structured meals.

TYPES OF WRAPS: FROM TORTILLAS TO LETTUCE LEAVES

The world of wraps is wonderfully diverse. Here are some of the most common types you'll encounter:

1. Flour Tortillas: The classic. Available in various sizes, these are versatile and easy to work with.

2. Corn Tortillas: Smaller and more fragile than flour tortillas, but packed with flavour. They're also gluten-free.

3. Whole Wheat Wraps: A healthier alternative to plain flour tortillas, with a slightly nutty flavour.

4. Spinach or Tomato Wraps: These colourful options can add a bit of flair to your meal.

5. Pita Bread: Not just for stuffing! When opened up, a pita makes a great wrap.

6. Lavash: This thin, soft flatbread is perfect for making roll-ups.

7. Lettuce Leaves: For a low-carb option, large lettuce leaves like romaine or butter lettuce work brilliantly.

8. Rice Paper: Used in Vietnamese cuisine, these become pliable when soaked in water.

9. Nori Sheets: These sheets of dried seaweed are traditional in sushi rolls but can be used creatively in other wraps too.

10. Cabbage Leaves: When blanched, these make a great wrap for heartier fillings.

CHOOSING THE RIGHT WRAP FOR YOUR MEAL

Selecting the right wrap can make or break your meal. Here are some factors to consider:

1. Filling Type: Hearty, saucy fillings need a sturdy wrap like a large flour tortilla. Lighter fillings can work with more delicate options like lettuce leaves.

2. Temperature: If you're making a hot wrap, choose something that can withstand heat without falling apart. Flour tortillas are great for this.

3. Flexibility: Some wraps, like corn tortillas, can crack if not warmed properly. If you're new to wrap-making, start with more forgiving options like flour tortillas.

4. Flavour Pairing: Consider how the wrap will complement your fillings. A nori sheet pairs wonderfully with Asian-inspired fillings, while a spinach wrap might clash with certain flavours.

5. Dietary Needs: Always keep in mind any dietary restrictions. There are gluten-free, low-carb, and grain-free options available.

STORING AND PRESERVING DIFFERENT WRAP TYPES

Proper storage is crucial to keep your wraps fresh and prevent waste. Here are some tips:

1. Flour and Corn Tortillas: Keep in an airtight bag or container at room temperature. They'll last about a week. For longer storage, freeze with parchment paper between each tortilla.

2. Pita and Lavash: Store in a bread bag at room temperature for a few days, or freeze for longer storage.

3. Lettuce and Cabbage Leaves: Wash, dry thoroughly, and store in the refrigerator in a plastic bag with a slightly damp paper towel. Use within a few days.

4. Rice Paper: Store in its original packaging in a cool, dry place. It will keep almost indefinitely.

5. Nori Sheets: Once opened, store in an airtight container with a desiccant packet. Keep in a cool, dry place.

Remember, freshness is key to a great wrap. Always check for signs of spoilage before using, and when in doubt, throw it out!

With this knowledge of equipment and wrap types, you're well on your way to becoming a wrap master. In the next sections, we'll dive into techniques and recipes that will have you creating wrap masterpieces in no time!

MASTERING WRAP TECHNIQUES

Now that we've covered the basics, it's time to dive into the heart of wrap-making. Mastering these techniques will take your wraps from good to absolutely brilliant. Don't worry if you don't get it right the first time – like any skill, practice makes perfect!

THE PERFECT FOLD: STEP-BY-STEP GUIDE

The key to a great wrap is in the fold. Here's my foolproof method:

1. Warm the wrap: This makes it more pliable and less likely to crack.

2. Place fillings in the centre: Leave about an inch of space around the edges.

3. Fold the bottom up: This creates a base for your fillings.

4. Fold in the sides: Tuck them in tightly around the fillings.

5. Roll from the bottom: Keep it tight as you go.

6. Secure the seam: Place the wrap seam-side down on your plate or secure it with a toothpick.

Remember, don't overstuff! It's tempting to pile on the fillings, but an overstuffed wrap is likely to fall apart.

ROLLING TECHNIQUES FOR DIFFERENT WRAP TYPES

Different wraps require different techniques. Here are a few key ones:

1. Burrito-style: Perfect for flour tortillas. Follow the steps above, but fold in both sides before rolling.

2. Open-ended: Great for pitas or lavash. Fold the bottom up and one side in, then roll.

3. Lettuce wraps: These are delicate, so go easy. Simply place fillings in the centre and fold the sides over.

4. Rice paper rolls: Soak the rice paper, place fillings in the centre, fold in the sides, and then roll tightly from the bottom.

5. Nori rolls: Place a sheet of nori on a bamboo mat, spread rice on top, add fillings, and use the mat to roll tightly.

COMMON MISTAKES AND HOW TO AVOID THEM

1. Overstuffing: Start with less filling than you think you need. You can always add more next time.

2. Uneven distribution: Spread your fillings evenly for a balanced bite every time.

3. Soggy wraps: Place wet ingredients (like tomatoes or sauces) in the centre, away from the wrap itself.

4. Tearing: Be gentle, especially with delicate wraps like corn tortillas or rice paper.

5. Not warming: Many wraps become more pliable when warmed. A quick zap in the microwave or on a dry pan can work wonders.

TROUBLESHOOTING WRAP ISSUES

Even the best wrap-makers encounter issues sometimes. Here's how to fix common problems:

1. Wrap breaks when folding: It might be too cold or dry. Try warming it or adding a bit of moisture with a damp paper towel.

2. Fillings fall out: You might be overstuffing. Try using less filling or double-wrapping.

3. Wrap is too dry: Add a sauce or dressing to moisten it up.

4. Wrap gets soggy quickly: Place wet ingredients in the centre and consider using a barrier like lettuce between moist fillings and the wrap.

5. Uneven cooking in hot wraps: Make sure your fillings are evenly distributed and at a similar temperature before wrapping.

Remember, every wrap is a learning experience. Don't be discouraged if your first few attempts aren't perfect – you'll be a pro in no time!

MEAL PLANNING AND PREP

One of the best things about wraps is how well they lend themselves to meal planning and prep. With a bit of forethought, you can set yourself up for a week of delicious, hassle-free meals.

PLANNING YOUR WEEK OF WRAPS

Here's how I approach planning a week of wraps:

1. Choose your wraps: Decide what types of wraps you'll use throughout the week.

2. Plan your proteins: I usually choose 2-3 proteins to prep in advance.

3. Select your veggies: Aim for a variety of colours and textures.

4. Don't forget the sauces: These can make or break your wrap. Plan for 2-3 different options.

5. Consider your schedule: Plan quicker wraps for busy days and more involved ones for when you have more time.

HERE'S A SAMPLE WEEKLY PLAN:

Monday: Greek-style chicken wraps
Tuesday: Veggie and hummus rolls
Wednesday: Breakfast burritos for dinner
Thursday: Thai-inspired prawn lettuce wraps
Friday: Build-your-own wrap night with leftover fillings

BATCH COOKING FOR EASY WRAP MEALS

Batch cooking is your secret weapon for easy-wrap meals. Here's what I typically prep on a Sunday:

1. Proteins: Grilled chicken, seasoned black beans, and boiled eggs are great options.

2. Roasted veggies: These are brilliant for adding flavour and can be used cold or reheated.

3. Sauces and dressings: Having these ready to go makes assembling wraps a breeze.

4. Grains: Cooked rice or quinoa can add substance to your wraps.

5. Chopped fresh veggies: Store these in airtight containers for quick assembly.

STORAGE AND REHEATING TIPS FOR MAKE-AHEAD WRAPS

Properly stored, make-ahead wraps can be a lifesaver on busy days. Here are my top tips:

1. Store components separately: This prevents soggy wraps. Assemble just before eating.

2. Use airtight containers: This keeps everything fresh longer.

3. Pat dry moist ingredients: This helps prevent sogginess.

4. Wrap in foil for reheating: This helps distribute heat evenly.

5. Reheat in the oven or on a dry pan: Microwaving can make wraps soggy.

6. Freeze with caution: Some wraps freeze well, others don't. Experiment to see what works for you.

Remember, not all wraps are created equal when it comes to make-ahead meals. Sturdy wraps like flour tortillas tend to hold up better than delicate options like lettuce leaves.

With these techniques and planning strategies in your arsenal, you're well on your way to becoming a wrap master. In the next sections, we'll dive into specific recipes that will put all of this knowledge into delicious practice. **HAPPY WRAPPING!**

CHAPTER 1: BREAKFAST WRAPS

CLASSIC ENGLISH BREAKFAST WRAP

Prep: 10 mins | **Cook:** 15 mins | **Serves:** 2
Cooking Function: Air Fry & Sauté

Ingredients:

UK: 2 large flour tortillas, 2 sausages (120g), 2 rashers of back bacon (100g), 2 large eggs, 100g baked beans, 50g grated cheddar cheese, 1 tablespoon olive oil, salt and pepper to taste

US: 2 large flour tortillas, 2 sausages (4 oz), 2 slices back bacon (3.5 oz), 2 large eggs, ½ cup baked beans, ½ cup shredded cheddar cheese, 1 tablespoon olive oil, salt and pepper to taste

Instructions:

1. Preheat the air fryer to 180°C (350°F) using the Air Fry function. Place the sausages inside and cook for 10 minutes, turning halfway.
2. While the sausages cook, heat a pan over medium heat with 1 tablespoon olive oil. Sauté the bacon for 2-3 minutes per side until crispy.
3. Crack the eggs into the same pan, season with salt and pepper, and cook sunny side up for about 2 minutes.
4. Warm the tortillas in the microwave or in a dry pan for 30 seconds to make them pliable.
5. Slice the cooked sausages and place them in the centre of each tortilla. Add the bacon, egg, a spoonful of baked beans, and a sprinkle of cheddar cheese.
6. Fold the sides of the tortilla inward and roll it up tightly into a wrap.
7. Place the wrapped tortillas back into the air fryer for 2-3 minutes to lightly toast and melt the cheese.
8. Serve immediately and enjoy a hearty breakfast on the go!

Nutrition Info (per wrap): Calories: 520 | Fat: 30g | Carbs: 34g | Protein: 25g

SMOKED SALMON AND CREAM CHEESE WRAP

Prep: 5 mins | **Cook:** 0 mins | **Serves:** 2
Cooking Function: None

Ingredients:

UK: 2 large flour tortillas, 100g smoked salmon, 100g cream cheese, 1 tablespoon lemon juice, ½ teaspoon black pepper, 20g fresh rocket leaves

US: 2 large flour tortillas, 3.5 oz smoked salmon, 3.5 oz cream cheese, 1 tablespoon lemon juice, ½ teaspoon black pepper, ½ cup arugula

Instructions:
1. In a bowl, mix the cream cheese with the lemon juice and black pepper until smooth.
2. Spread a generous layer of the cream cheese mixture across each tortilla.
3. Lay the smoked salmon slices evenly on top of the cream cheese.
4. Add a handful of rocket leaves to each wrap for a fresh bite.
5. Roll the tortillas tightly, slice them in half, and serve.
6. Perfect for a quick breakfast or brunch treat!

Nutrition Info (per wrap): Calories: 350 | Fat: 18g | Carbs: 30g | Protein: 20g

VEGGIE-PACKED OMELETTE WRAP

Prep: 10 mins | Cook: 10 mins | Serves: 2
Cooking Function: Sauté
Ingredients:

UK: 2 large flour tortillas, 4 large eggs, 50ml milk, 50g bell peppers (diced), 30g red onion (chopped), 30g spinach, 50g feta cheese, 1 tablespoon olive oil, salt and pepper

US: 2 large flour tortillas, 4 large eggs, ¼ cup milk, 1.75 oz bell peppers (diced), 1 oz red onion (chopped), 1 oz spinach, 1.75 oz feta cheese, 1 tablespoon olive oil, salt and pepper

Instructions:
1. In a bowl, whisk together the eggs, milk, salt, and pepper.
2. Heat the olive oil in a pan over medium heat and sauté the onions and bell peppers for 3-4 minutes.
3. Add the spinach and cook for 1 more minute until wilted.
4. Pour the egg mixture into the pan and stir gently until set but still soft.
5. Crumble the feta over the eggs and mix gently.
6. Warm the tortillas and spoon the omelette mixture evenly onto each one.
7. Roll up the wraps tightly and serve immediately.

Nutrition Info (per wrap): Calories: 400 | Fat: 22g | Carbs: 25g | Protein: 18g

PEANUT BUTTER AND BANANA BREAKFAST ROLL

Prep: 5 mins | **Cook:** 0 mins | **Serves:** 2
Cooking Function: None
Ingredients:

UK: 2 large whole wheat tortillas, 2 bananas, 4 tablespoons peanut butter, 1 tablespoon honey, 1 teaspoon chia seeds

US: 2 large whole wheat tortillas, 2 bananas, ¼ cup peanut butter, 1 tablespoon honey, 1 teaspoon chia seeds

Instructions:

1. Spread 2 tablespoons of peanut butter on each tortilla.
2. Peel the bananas and place one in the centre of each wrap.
3. Drizzle honey over the bananas and sprinkle chia seeds for added texture.
4. Roll the tortillas tightly and slice them in half for easy eating.

Nutrition Info (per wrap): Calories: 350 | Fat: 15g | Carbs: 45g | Protein: 10g

FULL ENGLISH BREAKFAST BURRITO

Prep: 10 mins | **Cook:** 15 mins | **Serves:** 2
Cooking Function: Air Fry
Ingredients:

UK: 2 large tortillas, 2 sausages, 2 rashers of bacon, 2 eggs, 100g baked beans, 50g mushrooms, 30g cheddar cheese, 1 tablespoon oil, salt and pepper

US: 2 large tortillas, 2 sausages, 2 slices bacon, 2 eggs, ½ cup baked beans, 1.75 oz mushrooms, ¼ cup cheddar, 1 tablespoon oil, salt and pepper

Instructions:

1. Cook the sausages and bacon in the air fryer at 180°C (350°F) for 10 minutes.
2. In a pan, sauté the mushrooms in oil until browned.
3. Fry the eggs sunny-side-up in the same pan.
4. Warm the tortillas, layer the ingredients, and roll them up burrito-style.

Nutrition Info (per wrap): Calories: 550 | Fat: 32g | Carbs: 38g | Protein: 24g

GREEK YOGURT AND BERRY BREAKFAST WRAP

Prep: 5 mins | Cook: 0 mins | Serves: 2
Cooking Function: None
Ingredients:

UK: 2 whole wheat tortillas, 200g Greek yoghurt, 100g mixed berries (strawberries, blueberries, raspberries), 1 tablespoon honey, 1 tablespoon chia seeds, 10g chopped almonds

US: 2 whole wheat tortillas, ¾ cup Greek yoghurt, ½ cup mixed berries, 1 tablespoon honey, 1 tablespoon chia seeds, 2 tablespoons chopped almonds

Instructions:
1. Spread 100g (½ cup) of Greek yoghurt onto each tortilla.
2. Add the mixed berries on top of the yoghurt, distributing evenly.
3. Drizzle with honey and sprinkle the chia seeds and almonds for extra crunch.
4. Roll the tortillas tightly, slice them in half, and enjoy straight away!

Nutrition Info (per wrap): Calories: 300 | Fat: 10g | Carbs: 38g | Protein: 12g

MUSHROOM AND SPINACH BREAKFAST QUESADILLA

Prep: 10 mins | Cook: 10 mins | Serves: 2
Cooking Function: Air Fry
Ingredients:

UK: 2 large tortillas, 100g mushrooms (sliced), 50g spinach, 1 garlic clove (minced), 80g grated mozzarella, 1 tablespoon olive oil, salt and pepper

US: 2 large tortillas, 3.5 oz mushrooms, 1.75 oz spinach, 1 garlic clove, ⅔ cup mozzarella, 1 tablespoon olive oil, salt and pepper

Instructions:
1. Preheat the air fryer to 180°C (350°F).
2. Sauté the mushrooms, garlic, and spinach in olive oil until the mushrooms are soft and the spinach wilts.
3. Spread the mixture evenly over one tortilla, sprinkle with mozzarella, and top with the second tortilla.
4. Place the quesadilla in the air fryer basket and cook for 4-5 minutes, flipping halfway, until golden and crisp.
5. Slice into quarters and serve warm.

Nutrition Info (per wrap): Calories: 380 | Fat: 18g | Carbs: 35g | Protein: 15g

HAM AND CHEESE BREAKFAST WRAP

Prep: 5 mins | **Cook:** 5 mins | **Serves:** 2
Cooking Function: Air Fry
Ingredients:
UK: 2 large tortillas, 100g sliced ham, 80g grated cheddar, 2 eggs, 1 tablespoon butter
US: 2 large tortillas, 3.5 oz sliced ham, ⅔ cup grated cheddar, 2 eggs, 1 tablespoon butter
Instructions:
1. Melt the butter in a pan and scramble the eggs lightly.
2. Place the ham and eggs onto the tortillas, sprinkle with cheddar, and roll them up.
3. Pop the wraps into the air fryer at 180°C (350°F) for 2-3 minutes to toast the tortillas and melt the cheese.

Nutrition Info (per wrap): Calories: 420 | Fat: 22g | Carbs: 28g | Protein: 22g

AVOCADO TOAST WRAP

Prep: 5 mins | **Cook:** 5 mins | **Serves:** 2
Cooking Function: None
Ingredients:
UK: 2 large tortillas, 2 ripe avocados, 1 teaspoon lemon juice, salt and pepper, 4 cherry tomatoes (halved), 10g pumpkin seeds
US: 2 large tortillas, 2 avocados, 1 teaspoon lemon juice, salt and pepper, 4 cherry tomatoes, 1 tablespoon pumpkin seeds
Instructions:
1. Mash the avocados with lemon juice, salt, and pepper.
2. Spread the mashed avocado onto each tortilla.
3. Add the cherry tomatoes and sprinkle with pumpkin seeds.
4. Roll up and enjoy a quick, nutritious breakfast.

Nutrition Info (per wrap): Calories: 350 | Fat: 26g | Carbs: 30g | Protein: 7g

SCRAMBLED TOFU BREAKFAST WRAP

Prep: 10 mins | **Cook:** 5 mins | **Serves:** 2
Cooking Function: Sauté
Ingredients:

UK: 2 large tortillas, 200g firm tofu (crumbled), ½ teaspoon turmeric, 1 tablespoon olive oil, 50g spinach, 50g cherry tomatoes (halved), salt and pepper

US: 2 large tortillas, 7 oz firm tofu, ½ teaspoon turmeric, 1 tablespoon olive oil, 1.75 oz spinach, 1.75 oz cherry tomatoes, salt and pepper

Instructions:

1. Heat the olive oil in a pan and sauté the tofu with turmeric, salt, and pepper for 3-4 minutes.
2. Add the spinach and tomatoes and cook for another minute.
3. Spoon the tofu scramble onto the tortillas, roll them up, and enjoy.

Nutrition Info (per wrap): Calories: 280 | Fat: 14g | Carbs: 25g | Protein: 15g

NUTELLA AND STRAWBERRY CREPE WRAP

Prep: 5 mins | **Cook:** 5 mins | **Serves:** 2
Cooking Function: None
Ingredients:

UK: 2 large crepes, 4 tablespoons Nutella, 100g strawberries (sliced)

US: 2 large crepes, ¼ cup Nutella, 3.5 oz strawberries

Instructions:

1. Spread Nutella over each crepe.
2. Add the sliced strawberries on top.
3. Roll up the crepes and serve immediately.

Nutrition Info (per wrap): Calories: 320 | Fat: 12g | Carbs: 45g | Protein: 6g

BACON, EGG, AND CHEESE WRAP

Prep: 5 mins | Cook: 10 mins | Serves: 2
Cooking Function: Air Fry
Ingredients:
UK: 2 large tortillas, 4 rashers of bacon, 2 eggs, 50g grated cheddar, salt and pepper
US: 2 large tortillas, 4 slices bacon, 2 eggs, ¼ cup cheddar, salt and pepper
Instructions:
1. Cook the bacon in the air fryer at 180°C (350°F) for 8 minutes.
2. Fry the eggs in a pan, seasoning with salt and pepper.
3. Place the bacon, eggs, and cheese onto the tortillas and roll them up.
4. Return the wraps to the air fryer for 2-3 minutes to melt the cheese.

Nutrition Info (per wrap): Calories: 450 | Fat: 28g | Carbs: 28g | Protein: 22g

APPLE AND CINNAMON BREAKFAST BURRITO

Prep: 5 mins | Cook: 10 mins | Serves: 2
Cooking Function: Sauté
Ingredients:

UK: 2 large tortillas, 2 apples (peeled and sliced), 1 teaspoon cinnamon, 1 tablespoon butter, 1 tablespoon honey

US: 2 large tortillas, 2 apples, 1 teaspoon cinnamon, 1 tablespoon butter, 1 tablespoon honey

Instructions:

1. Melt the butter in a pan and sauté the apple slices with cinnamon for 5 minutes.
2. Drizzle honey over the apples and cook for 1 more minute.
3. Spoon the apples onto the tortillas, roll them up, and enjoy warm.

Nutrition Info (per wrap): Calories: 320 | Fat: 8g | Carbs: 55g | Protein: 4g

CHAPTER 2: LUNCH BOX HEROES

CLASSIC CHICKEN CAESAR WRAP

Prep: 10 mins | Cook: 5 mins | Serves: 2
Cooking Function: Reheat
Ingredients:

UK: 2 large tortillas, 200g cooked chicken breast (sliced), 50g romaine lettuce, 30g grated Parmesan, 2 tablespoons Caesar dressing, salt and pepper

US: 2 large tortillas, 7 oz cooked chicken breast, 2 oz romaine lettuce, ¼ cup grated Parmesan, 2 tablespoons Caesar dressing, salt and pepper

Instructions:

1. Preheat the air fryer to 160°C (320°F) using the Reheat function and warm the tortillas for 2 minutes.
2. In a bowl, toss the chicken, lettuce, Parmesan, and Caesar dressing. Season with salt and pepper.
3. Divide the mixture between the tortillas and wrap tightly.
4. Slice in half and enjoy immediately, or store for later in the fridge.

Nutrition Info (per wrap): Calories: 380 | Fat: 18g | Carbs: 25g | Protein: 30g

TUNA SALAD WRAP

Prep: 5 mins | Cook: 0 mins | Serves: 2
Cooking Function: No cooking required
Ingredients:

UK: 2 large tortillas, 160g canned tuna (drained), 2 tablespoons mayonnaise, ½ red onion (finely chopped), 1 celery stick (diced), 50g lettuce leaves, salt and pepper

US: 2 large tortillas, 6 oz canned tuna, 2 tablespoons mayonnaise, ½ red onion, 1 celery stick, 2 oz lettuce leaves, salt and pepper

Instructions:

1. Mix the tuna, mayonnaise, onion, and celery in a bowl. Season with salt and pepper.
2. Lay the tortillas flat and place some lettuce on each.
3. Spoon the tuna mixture evenly over the lettuce.
4. Wrap tightly and serve immediately, or refrigerate for a quick lunch later.

Nutrition Info (per wrap): Calories: 350 | Fat: 12g | Carbs: 28g | Protein: 25g

MEDITERRANEAN HUMMUS AND FALAFEL WRAP

Prep: 10 mins | **Cook:** 5 mins | **Serves:** 2
Cooking Function: Air Fry
Ingredients:
UK: 2 large tortillas, 100g hummus, 4 falafel balls, 50g spinach, 4 cherry tomatoes (halved), 1 tablespoon tahini, salt and pepper
US: 2 large tortillas, ½ cup hummus, 4 falafel balls, 2 oz spinach, 4 cherry tomatoes, 1 tablespoon tahini, salt and pepper
Instructions:
1. Air fry the falafel at 180°C (350°F) for 5 minutes until crispy.
2. Spread hummus evenly over each tortilla, then top with spinach and falafel.
3. Add the halved cherry tomatoes and drizzle with tahini. Season lightly with salt and pepper.
4. Wrap, slice, and enjoy!

Nutrition Info (per wrap): Calories: 400 | Fat: 18g | Carbs: 40g | Protein: 15g

TURKEY AND CRANBERRY WRAP

Prep: 5 mins | **Cook:** 2 mins | **Serves:** 2
Cooking Function: Reheat
Ingredients:
UK: 2 large tortillas, 200g sliced turkey breast, 2 tablespoons cranberry sauce, 50g rocket leaves, 30g cream cheese
US: 2 large tortillas, 7 oz sliced turkey breast, 2 tablespoons cranberry sauce, 2 oz rocket leaves, 2 tablespoons cream cheese
Instructions:
1. Preheat the air fryer to 160°C (320°F) and warm the tortillas for 2 minutes.
2. Spread cream cheese over each tortilla.
3. Layer the turkey slices and rocket leaves, and top with a spoonful of cranberry sauce.
4. Wrap tightly, slice, and enjoy!

Nutrition Info (per wrap): Calories: 360 | Fat: 12g | Carbs: 30g | Protein: 28g

EGG MAYONNAISE AND CRESS WRAP

Prep: 10 mins | **Cook:** 10 mins | **Serves:** 2
Cooking Function: Boil
Ingredients:
UK: 2 large tortillas, 4 boiled eggs, 2 tablespoons mayonnaise, 1 tablespoon Dijon mustard, 20g cress, salt and pepper
US: 2 large tortillas, 4 boiled eggs, 2 tablespoons mayonnaise, 1 tablespoon Dijon mustard, ¾ oz cress, salt and pepper
Instructions:
1. Boil the eggs for 8-10 minutes, then cool and peel.
2. Mash the eggs in a bowl and mix in the mayonnaise, mustard, salt, and pepper.
3. Spread the egg mixture onto each tortilla and sprinkle with cress.
4. Roll up, slice, and enjoy fresh or packed for later.

Nutrition Info (per wrap): Calories: 300 | Fat: 18g | Carbs: 20g | Protein: 14g

BLT (BACON, LETTUCE, TOMATO) WRAP

Prep: 5 mins | **Cook:** 10 mins | **Serves:** 2
Cooking Function: Air Fry
Ingredients:
UK: 2 large tortillas, 4 rashers of bacon, 50g lettuce, 2 tomatoes (sliced), 1 tablespoon mayonnaise
US: 2 large tortillas, 4 slices bacon, 2 oz lettuce, 2 tomatoes, 1 tablespoon mayonnaise
Instructions:
1. Air fry the bacon at 180°C (350°F) for 8-10 minutes until crispy.
2. Spread mayonnaise on each tortilla, then layer the lettuce, bacon, and tomato slices.
3. Wrap, slice, and enjoy hot or cold!

Nutrition Info (per wrap): Calories: 400 | Fat: 25g | Carbs: 25g | Protein: 20g

CORONATION CHICKEN WRAP

Prep: 10 mins | **Cook:** 0 mins | **Serves:** 2
Cooking Function: No cooking required
Ingredients:

UK: 2 large tortillas, 200g cooked chicken, 2 tablespoons mayonnaise, 1 teaspoon curry powder, 1 tablespoon raisins, 1 tablespoon almonds (sliced)

US: 2 large tortillas, 7 oz cooked chicken, 2 tablespoons mayonnaise, 1 teaspoon curry powder, 1 tablespoon raisins, 1 tablespoon almonds

Instructions:

1. Mix the chicken, mayonnaise, curry powder, raisins, and almonds in a bowl.
2. Spread the mixture evenly over each tortilla and wrap.
3. Slice in half and enjoy straight away or refrigerate.

Nutrition Info (per wrap): Calories: 370 | Fat: 18g | Carbs: 30g | Protein: 28g

PLOUGHMAN'S LUNCH WRAP

Prep: 10 mins | **Cook:** 0 mins | **Serves:** 2
Cooking Function: No cooking required
Ingredients:

UK: 2 large tortillas, 100g mature cheddar cheese (sliced), 50g cooked ham (sliced), 1 small apple (sliced), 50g pickled onions, 1 tablespoon wholegrain mustard, a handful of mixed salad leaves

US: 2 large tortillas, 3.5 oz mature cheddar cheese, 2 oz cooked ham, 1 small apple, 2 oz pickled onions, 1 tablespoon wholegrain mustard, a handful of mixed salad leaves

Instructions:

1. Lay the tortillas flat and spread the wholegrain mustard evenly over each.
2. Layer the cheese, ham, apple slices, pickled onions, and mixed salad leaves on top.
3. Roll up tightly and cut in half. Enjoy fresh or pack for a delightful lunch!

Nutrition Info (per wrap): Calories: 420 | Fat: 22g | Carbs: 38g | Protein: 22g

PRAWN AND AVOCADO WRAP

Prep: 5 mins | Cook: 0 mins | Serves: 2
Cooking Function: No cooking required
Ingredients:
UK: 2 large tortillas, 150g cooked prawns, 1 avocado (sliced), 50g lettuce, juice of 1 lime, salt and pepper
US: 2 large tortillas, 5 oz cooked prawns, 1 avocado, 2 oz lettuce, juice of 1 lime, salt and pepper
Instructions:
1. In a bowl, mix the cooked prawns with lime juice, salt, and pepper.
2. Spread the prawns evenly over each tortilla.
3. Top with sliced avocado and lettuce.
4. Wrap tightly, slice, and enjoy!

Nutrition Info (per wrap): Calories: 350 | Fat: 20g | Carbs: 30g | Protein: 18g

ROAST BEEF AND HORSERADISH WRAP

Prep: 5 mins | Cook: 0 mins | Serves: 2
Cooking Function: No cooking required
Ingredients:
UK: 2 large tortillas, 200g roast beef (sliced), 1 tablespoon horseradish sauce, 50g rocket leaves, 1 small red onion (thinly sliced)
US: 2 large tortillas, 7 oz roast beef, 1 tablespoon horseradish sauce, 2 oz rocket leaves, 1 small red onion
Instructions:
1. Spread horseradish sauce evenly over each tortilla.
2. Layer the roast beef, rocket leaves, and red onion on top.
3. Roll up tightly and cut in half for a satisfying lunch!

Nutrition Info (per wrap): Calories: 420 | Fat: 20g | Carbs: 30g | Protein: 35g

GREEK SALAD WRAP

Prep: 10 mins | **Cook:** 0 mins | **Serves:** 2

Cooking Function: No cooking required

Ingredients:

UK: 2 large tortillas, 100g feta cheese (crumbled), 1 cucumber (diced), 2 tomatoes (diced), 50g kalamata olives (pitted), 1 tablespoon olive oil, 1 teaspoon dried oregano

US: 2 large tortillas, 3.5 oz feta cheese, 1 cucumber, 2 tomatoes, 2 oz kalamata olives, 1 tablespoon olive oil, 1 teaspoon dried oregano

Instructions:

1. In a bowl, combine the feta, cucumber, tomatoes, olives, olive oil, and oregano.
2. Spoon the mixture onto each tortilla.
3. Wrap tightly, slice, and enjoy this refreshing Greek-inspired meal!

Nutrition Info (per wrap): Calories: 350 | Fat: 25g | Carbs: 20g | Protein: 10g

PESTO CHICKEN AND MOZZARELLA WRAP

Prep: 10 mins | **Cook:** 5 mins | **Serves:** 2

Cooking Function: Air Fry

Ingredients:

UK: 2 large tortillas, 200g cooked chicken (sliced), 100g mozzarella cheese (sliced), 2 tablespoons pesto, 50g spinach

US: 2 large tortillas, 7 oz cooked chicken, 3.5 oz mozzarella cheese, 2 tablespoons pesto, 2 oz spinach

Instructions:

1. Preheat the air fryer to 180°C (350°F).
2. Spread pesto on each tortilla.
3. Layer the chicken, mozzarella, and spinach on top.
4. Roll tightly and place in the air fryer for 5 minutes until heated through and the cheese is melted.
5. Slice and serve warm!

Nutrition Info (per wrap): Calories: 450 | Fat: 25g | Carbs: 30g | Protein: 30g

CURRIED EGG SALAD WRAP

Prep: 10 mins | **Cook:** 0 mins | **Serves:** 2
Cooking Function: No cooking required
Ingredients:

UK: 2 large tortillas, 4 hard-boiled eggs (chopped), 2 tablespoons mayonnaise, 1 teaspoon curry powder, 1 tablespoon chopped fresh coriander, salt and pepper

US: 2 large tortillas, 4 hard-boiled eggs, 2 tablespoons mayonnaise, 1 teaspoon curry powder, 1 tablespoon chopped fresh cilantro, salt and pepper

Instructions:

1. In a bowl, mix the chopped eggs, mayonnaise, curry powder, coriander, salt, and pepper.
2. Spread the egg salad over each tortilla.
3. Wrap tightly, slice in half, and enjoy!

Nutrition Info (per wrap): Calories: 310 | Fat: 18g | Carbs: 20g | Protein: 14g

CHAPTER 3: DINNER DELIGHTS

SPICY BEEF AND BEAN BURRITO

Prep: 15 mins | Cook: 20 mins | Serves: 4
Cooking Function: Air Fry
Ingredients:

UK: 500g minced beef, 400g canned black beans (drained and rinsed), 1 onion (chopped), 2 cloves garlic (minced), 1 tablespoon chilli powder, 1 teaspoon cumin, 4 large tortillas, 100g cheddar cheese (grated), salt and pepper to taste

US: 1.1 lbs minced beef, 14 oz canned black beans, 1 onion, 2 cloves garlic, 1 tablespoon chilli powder, 1 teaspoon cumin, 4 large tortillas, 3.5 oz cheddar cheese, salt and pepper to taste

Instructions:

1. In a frying pan over medium heat, brown the minced beef until cooked through. Drain excess fat.
2. Add the chopped onion and minced garlic, and sauté for about 3 minutes until softened.
3. Stir in the chilli powder, cumin, black beans, salt, and pepper. Cook for an additional 5 minutes until heated through.
4. Place a generous scoop of the beef and bean mixture on each tortilla, sprinkle with cheddar cheese, and roll them up tightly.
5. Preheat the air fryer to 180°C (350°F). Place the burritos in the air fryer basket and cook for 10 minutes until crispy.
6. Remove and serve warm, with your favourite salsa or guacamole.

Nutrition Info (per burrito): Calories: 450 | Fat: 24g | Carbs: 30g | Protein: 28g

CRISPY DUCK PANCAKES

Prep: 15 mins | Cook: 30 mins | Serves: 4
Cooking Function: Air Fry
Ingredients:

UK: 400g duck breast, 8 Chinese pancakes, 100g cucumber (julienned), 100g spring onions (julienned), hoisin sauce for drizzling

US: 0.9 lbs duck breast, 8 Chinese pancakes, 3.5 oz cucumber, 3.5 oz spring onions, hoisin sauce

Instructions:
1. Score the skin of the duck breast and season with salt and pepper. Place skin-side down in a cold frying pan, then turn the heat to medium. Cook for about 8-10 minutes until the skin is crispy.
2. Flip the duck and cook for another 5-8 minutes until cooked to your liking. Allow to rest for 5 minutes, then slice thinly.
3. Warm the Chinese pancakes according to package instructions.
4. To assemble, place slices of duck, cucumber, and spring onions on a pancake, drizzle with hoisin sauce, and wrap it up.
5. Serve immediately and enjoy the crispy texture!

Nutrition Info (per pancake): Calories: 350 | Fat: 20g | Carbs: 30g | Protein: 20g

FISH AND CHIPS WRAP

Prep: 10 mins | Cook: 15 mins | Serves: 2
Cooking Function: Air Fry

Ingredients:

UK: 2 large tortillas, 300g battered fish fillets (cooked), 150g chips (cooked), 50g tartar sauce, lemon wedges for serving

US: 2 large tortillas, 10.5 oz battered fish fillets, 5.3 oz chips, 1.8 oz tartar sauce, lemon wedges

Instructions:
1. Cook the battered fish and chips in the air fryer according to package instructions until crispy and hot.
2. Place the cooked fish and chips onto each tortilla.
3. Drizzle with tartar sauce and squeeze fresh lemon juice over the top.
4. Wrap tightly and enjoy a classic fish and chips meal in a convenient form!

Nutrition Info (per wrap): Calories: 600 | Fat: 32g | Carbs: 56g | Protein: 24g

LAMB KOFTA WRAP WITH TZATZIKI

Prep: 15 mins | **Cook:** 20 mins | **Serves:** 4
Cooking Function: Grill
Ingredients:

UK: 500g minced lamb, 2 cloves garlic (minced), 1 teaspoon ground cumin, 1 teaspoon ground coriander, 1 teaspoon paprika, salt and pepper to taste, 4 large flatbreads, 100g tzatziki, mixed salad leaves

US: 1.1 lbs minced lamb, 2 cloves garlic, 1 teaspoon ground cumin, 1 teaspoon ground coriander, 1 teaspoon paprika, 4 large flatbreads, 3.5 oz tzatziki, mixed salad leaves

Instructions:

1. In a bowl, combine minced lamb, garlic, cumin, coriander, paprika, salt, and pepper. Mix well and shape into kofta (sausage-shaped) pieces.
2. Preheat your grill to medium-high. Cook the kofta for about 8-10 minutes, turning occasionally until cooked through.
3. Warm the flatbreads on the grill for a minute on each side.
4. To assemble, place a few koftas on each flatbread, top with tzatziki and mixed salad leaves, and then wrap it up.
5. Serve immediately for a delicious, flavour-packed dinner!

Nutrition Info (per wrap): Calories: 450 | Fat: 30g | Carbs: 30g | Protein: 25g

VEGETABLE STIR-FRY LETTUCE WRAPS

Prep: 10 mins | **Cook:** 5 mins | **Serves:** 4
Cooking Function: Stir Fry
Ingredients:

UK: 200g mixed bell peppers (sliced), 100g mushrooms (sliced), 1 courgette (sliced), 1 tablespoon soy sauce, 1 tablespoon sesame oil, 8 large lettuce leaves

US: 7 oz mixed bell peppers, 3.5 oz mushrooms, 1 courgette, 1 tablespoon soy sauce, 1 tablespoon sesame oil, 8 large lettuce leaves

Instructions:
1. Heat sesame oil in a frying pan over high heat. Add bell peppers, mushrooms, and courgette, and stir-fry for about 5 minutes until tender.
2. Drizzle with soy sauce and toss to combine.
3. Spoon the vegetable mixture into individual lettuce leaves to create wraps.
4. Serve immediately for a light and healthy dinner!

Nutrition Info (per wrap): Calories: 120 | Fat: 7g | Carbs: 12g | Protein: 3g

BBQ PULLED PORK WRAP

Prep: 10 mins | Cook: 5 hours | Serves: 4
Cooking Function: Slow Cook
Ingredients:
UK: 500g pork shoulder, 200ml BBQ sauce, 4 large tortillas, 100g coleslaw, salt and pepper to taste
US: 1.1 lbs pork shoulder, 0.8 cup BBQ sauce, 4 large tortillas, 3.5 oz coleslaw, salt and pepper

Instructions:
1. Season the pork shoulder with salt and pepper and place it in the slow cooker. Pour BBQ sauce over the top.
2. Cook on low for 5 hours until the pork is tender and easily pulled apart.
3. Remove the pork, shred it with forks, and mix it back into the sauce.
4. Warm the tortillas in the microwave or on a skillet.
5. Fill each tortilla with pulled pork and coleslaw, then wrap tightly. Serve warm!

Nutrition Info (per wrap): Calories: 550 | Fat: 28g | Carbs: 40g | Protein: 32g

CHICKEN TIKKA MASALA WRAP

Prep: 10 mins | **Cook:** 20 mins | **Serves:** 2
Cooking Function: Air Fry
Ingredients:
UK: 400g chicken breast (diced), 150g tikka masala sauce, 2 large tortillas, 50g yoghurt, 100g cucumber (sliced)
US: 0.9 lbs chicken breast, 5.3 oz tikka masala sauce, 2 large tortillas, 1.8 oz yoghurt, 3.5 oz cucumber
Instructions:
1. In a bowl, toss the chicken pieces with tikka masala sauce until well coated.
2. Preheat the air fryer to 200°C (400°F). Cook the chicken for about 10-12 minutes until cooked through.
3. Warm the tortillas and spread yoghurt on each.
4. Add the cooked chicken and sliced cucumber, then wrap up. Enjoy this tasty twist on tikka masala!

Nutrition Info (per wrap): Calories: 450 | Fat: 15g | Carbs: 40g | Protein: 40g

FAJITA-STYLE STEAK WRAP

Prep: 10 mins | **Cook:** 15 mins | **Serves:** 2
Cooking Function: Grill
Ingredients:
UK: 300g steak (sliced), 1 bell pepper (sliced), 1 onion (sliced), 2 tablespoons fajita seasoning, 2 large tortillas
US: 0.7 lbs steak, 1 bell pepper, 1 onion, 2 tablespoons fajita seasoning, 2 large tortillas
Instructions:
1. In a bowl, mix sliced steak with fajita seasoning.
2. Heat your grill to high, and add the steak, bell pepper, and onion, cooking for about 8-10 minutes until the steak is done and the veggies are tender.
3. Warm the tortillas on the grill.
4. Fill each tortilla with the steak and veggie mixture, then wrap it up and enjoy the zesty flavours!

Nutrition Info (per wrap): Calories: 500 | Fat: 20g | Carbs: 35g | Protein: 40g

SPINACH AND RICOTTA CANNELLONI WRAP

Prep: 20 mins | **Cook:** 25 mins | **Serves:** 4

Cooking Function: Bake

Ingredients:

UK: 250g spinach (cooked), 250g ricotta cheese, 8 cannelloni tubes, 400g tomato sauce, 100g mozzarella cheese (grated), salt and pepper to taste

US: 9 oz spinach, 9 oz ricotta cheese, 8 cannelloni tubes, 14 oz tomato sauce, 3.5 oz mozzarella cheese, salt and pepper

Instructions:

1. Preheat the oven to 180°C (350°F).
2. In a bowl, mix cooked spinach with ricotta cheese, salt, and pepper. Stuff the cannelloni tubes with this mixture.
3. Spread a thin layer of tomato sauce in a baking dish. Place the filled cannelloni on top and cover with the remaining sauce.
4. Sprinkle with mozzarella cheese and bake for 25 minutes until golden and bubbling.
5. Serve hot for a comforting meal!

Nutrition Info (per wrap): Calories: 380 | Fat: 18g | Carbs: 40g | Protein: 15g

TERIYAKI TOFU WRAP

Prep: 10 mins | **Cook:** 15 mins | **Serves:** 2

Cooking Function: Air Fry

Ingredients:

UK: 300g firm tofu (cubed), 50ml teriyaki sauce, 2 large tortillas, 100g mixed vegetables (stir-fried), sesame seeds for garnish

US: 0.7 lbs firm tofu, 1.7 oz teriyaki sauce, 2 large tortillas, 3.5 oz mixed vegetables, sesame seeds

Instructions:

1. Marinate the tofu cubes in teriyaki sauce for at least 10 minutes.
2. Preheat the air fryer to 180°C (350°F). Place marinated tofu in the air fryer and cook for 12-15 minutes until golden and crispy.
3. Warm the tortillas and fill them with cooked tofu and stir-fried vegetables.
4. Sprinkle with sesame seeds, wrap up, and enjoy this flavour-packed meal!

Nutrition Info (per wrap): Calories: 300 | Fat: 16g | Carbs: 30g | Protein: 18g

SAUSAGE AND MASH WRAP

Prep: 15 mins | **Cook:** 15 mins | **Serves:** 2
Cooking Function: Air Fry
Ingredients:
UK: 400g sausages, 200g mashed potatoes, 2 large tortillas, 50ml gravy, salt and pepper to taste
US: 0.9 lbs sausages, 7 oz mashed potatoes, 2 large tortillas, 1.7 oz gravy
Instructions:
1. Cook the sausages in the air fryer until golden brown and cooked through (about 12 minutes).
2. Warm the mashed potatoes and season with salt and pepper.
3. Lay tortillas flat, add a scoop of mashed potatoes and 2 sausages, then drizzle with gravy.
4. Wrap tightly and enjoy this comforting dish!

Nutrition Info (per wrap): Calories: 480 | Fat: 25g | Carbs: 40g | Protein: 20g

VEGETARIAN CHILLI WRAP

Prep: 10 mins | **Cook:** 25 mins | **Serves:** 4
Cooking Function: Cook
Ingredients:
UK: 400g canned kidney beans (drained), 400g canned chopped tomatoes, 1 onion (chopped), 1 bell pepper (chopped), 2 teaspoons chilli powder, 4 large tortillas, 50g grated cheese
US: 14 oz canned kidney beans, 14 oz canned chopped tomatoes, 1 onion, 1 bell pepper, 2 teaspoons chilli powder, 4 large tortillas, 1.8 oz grated cheese
Instructions:
1. In a pot, sauté the onion and bell pepper over medium heat for 5 minutes.
2. Add kidney beans, chopped tomatoes, and chilli powder. Simmer for about 15 minutes.
3. Warm the tortillas and fill with the chilli mixture, sprinkling cheese on top.
4. Wrap up and enjoy a hearty vegetarian meal!

Nutrition Info (per wrap): Calories: 350 | Fat: 10g | Carbs: 50g | Protein: 15g

MOROCCAN LAMB WRAP

Prep: 15 mins | **Cook:** 20 mins | **Serves:** 4

Cooking Function: Grill

Ingredients:

UK: 500g lamb mince, 1 teaspoon ground cinnamon, 1 teaspoon ground cumin, 1 teaspoon paprika, 4 large flatbreads, 100g hummus, mixed salad leaves

US: 1.1 lbs lamb mince, 1 teaspoon ground cinnamon, 1 teaspoon ground cumin, 1 teaspoon paprika, 4 large flatbreads, 3.5 oz hummus, mixed salad leaves

Instructions:

1. In a bowl, mix lamb mince with spices, salt, and pepper. Shape into small patties.
2. Preheat the grill and cook patties for about 10-15 minutes until cooked through.
3. Warm the flatbreads on the grill.
4. Spread hummus on each flatbread, add lamb patties and salad leaves, then wrap up. Enjoy the rich flavours!

Nutrition Info (per wrap): Calories: 460 | Fat: 25g | Carbs: 40g | Protein: 30g

CHAPTER 4: VEGETARIAN AND VEGAN DELIGHTS

FALAFEL AND HUMMUS WRAP

Prep: 15 mins | **Cook:** 25 mins | **Serves:** 2
Cooking Function: Air Fry

Ingredients:

UK: 200g canned chickpeas (drained and rinsed), 50g breadcrumbs, 1 tablespoon tahini, 1 teaspoon ground cumin, 1 teaspoon garlic powder, 1 teaspoon paprika, salt and pepper to taste, 4 large wraps, 100g hummus, mixed salad leaves

US: 7 oz canned chickpeas, 1.8 oz breadcrumbs, 1 tablespoon tahini, 1 teaspoon ground cumin, 1 teaspoon garlic powder, 1 teaspoon paprika, salt and pepper to taste, 4 large wraps, 3.5 oz hummus, mixed salad leaves

Instructions:

1. In a bowl, mash the chickpeas with a fork until mostly smooth.
2. Mix in breadcrumbs, tahini, cumin, garlic powder, paprika, salt, and pepper. Form the mixture into small balls.
3. Preheat the air fryer to 180°C (350°F). Place falafel balls in the basket and cook for about 15 minutes, shaking halfway through.
4. Spread hummus over each wrap and layer with mixed salad leaves.
5. Top with crispy falafel, wrap tightly, and enjoy this tasty, plant-based meal!

Nutrition Info (per wrap): Calories: 380 | Fat: 12g | Carbs: 54g | Protein: 12g

GRILLED HALLOUMI AND ROASTED VEGETABLE WRAP

Prep: 10 mins | **Cook:** 20 mins | **Serves:** 2
Cooking Function: Grill

Ingredients:

UK: 200g halloumi cheese (sliced), 1 courgette (sliced), 1 red bell pepper (sliced), 1 tablespoon olive oil, salt and pepper to taste, 2 large wraps, 50g pesto

US: 7 oz halloumi cheese, 1 courgette, 1 red bell pepper, 1 tablespoon olive oil, salt and pepper, 2 large wraps, 1.8 oz pesto

Instructions:
1. Preheat your grill to medium-high heat.
2. Toss courgette and bell pepper slices with olive oil, salt, and pepper. Grill for about 10 minutes until tender.
3. Meanwhile, grill halloumi slices for 2-3 minutes on each side until golden.
4. Spread pesto on each wrap, and layer with grilled vegetables and halloumi.
5. Wrap tightly and dig into this deliciously cheesy delight!

Nutrition Info (per wrap): Calories: 420 | Fat: 24g | Carbs: 30g | Protein: 22g

VEGAN 'CHICKEN' CAESAR WRAP

Prep: 15 mins | Cook: 10 mins | Serves: 2
Cooking Function: Air Fry

Ingredients:
UK: 200g vegan chicken strips, 50g romaine lettuce (shredded), 30g vegan Caesar dressing, 4 large wraps, 20g nutritional yeast (for topping)

US: 7 oz vegan chicken strips, 1.8 oz romaine lettuce, 1.1 oz vegan Caesar dressing, 4 large wraps, 0.7 oz nutritional yeast

Instructions:
1. Preheat the air fryer to 200°C (400°F).
2. Cook the vegan chicken strips for about 8-10 minutes until golden and crispy.
3. In a bowl, toss shredded lettuce with vegan Caesar dressing.
4. Spread the lettuce mixture on each wrap, top with crispy vegan chicken, and sprinkle with nutritional yeast.
5. Wrap it up and savour this creamy, plant-based treat!

Nutrition Info (per wrap): Calories: 350 | Fat: 10g | Carbs: 40g | Protein: 20g

SPICY BEAN AND GUACAMOLE BURRITO

Prep: 10 mins | **Cook:** 15 mins | **Serves:** 2

Cooking Function: Cook

Ingredients:

UK: 200g canned mixed beans (drained), 1 teaspoon chilli powder, 1 teaspoon cumin, salt to taste, 4 large wraps, 100g guacamole, 50g salsa

US: 7 oz canned mixed beans, 1 teaspoon chilli powder, 1 teaspoon cumin, salt, 4 large wraps, 3.5 oz guacamole, 1.8 oz salsa

Instructions:

1. In a pan, heat the mixed beans with chilli powder, cumin, and salt for about 5 minutes.
2. Warm the wraps in the microwave for a few seconds.
3. Spread guacamole over each wrap, then add the spicy bean mixture and salsa.
4. Wrap it up tightly and enjoy this flavour-packed burrito!

Nutrition Info (per wrap): Calories: 390 | Fat: 12g | Carbs: 54g | Protein: 15g

ROASTED BUTTERNUT SQUASH AND SAGE WRAP

Prep: 15 mins | **Cook:** 30 mins | **Serves:** 2

Cooking Function: Bake

Ingredients:

UK: 200g butternut squash (peeled and cubed), 1 tablespoon olive oil, 1 teaspoon dried sage, salt and pepper, 2 large wraps, 50g cream cheese

US: 7 oz butternut squash, 1 tablespoon olive oil, 1 teaspoon dried sage, salt and pepper, 2 large wraps, 1.8 oz cream cheese

Instructions:

1. Preheat the oven to 200°C (400°F).
2. Toss butternut squash cubes with olive oil, sage, salt, and pepper. Roast for 25 minutes until tender.
3. Spread cream cheese over each wrap, layer with roasted squash, and wrap tightly.
4. Enjoy the warm, creamy flavours of this hearty wrap!

Nutrition Info (per wrap): Calories: 420 | Fat: 20g | Carbs: 45g | Protein: 10g

VEGAN 'EGG' MAYO WRAP

Prep: 10 mins | **Cook:** 5 mins | **Serves:** 2
Cooking Function: Cook
Ingredients:
UK: 200g silken tofu (drained), 1 tablespoon nutritional yeast, 1 teaspoon mustard, salt and pepper to taste, 2 large wraps, 50g lettuce
US: 7 oz silken tofu, 1 tablespoon nutritional yeast, 1 teaspoon mustard, salt and pepper, 2 large wraps, 1.8 oz lettuce
Instructions:
1. In a bowl, mash silken tofu with nutritional yeast, mustard, salt, and pepper until creamy.
2. Spread the mixture over each wrap, and top with lettuce.
3. Wrap it up and enjoy this easy, protein-packed meal!

Nutrition Info (per wrap): Calories: 270 | Fat: 14g | Carbs: 25g | Protein: 10g

MUSHROOM SHAWARMA WRAP

Prep: 10 mins | **Cook:** 15 mins | **Serves:** 2
Cooking Function: Air Fry
Ingredients:
UK: 200g mushrooms (sliced), 2 teaspoons shawarma spice blend, 4 large wraps, 100g tzatziki sauce, mixed salad leaves
US: 7 oz mushrooms, 2 teaspoons shawarma spice blend, 4 large wraps, 3.5 oz tzatziki sauce, mixed salad leaves
Instructions:
1. In a bowl, toss mushrooms with shawarma spices.
2. Preheat the air fryer to 200°C (400°F). Cook mushrooms for about 10 minutes until golden.
3. Spread tzatziki on each wrap, add salad leaves, and top with cooked mushrooms.
4. Wrap it up and dive into this flavourful delight!

Nutrition Info (per wrap): Calories: 320 | Fat: 10g | Carbs: 38g | Protein: 12g

CHICKPEA 'TUNA' SALAD WRAP

Prep: 10 mins | **Cook:** 0 mins | **Serves:** 2
Cooking Function: None
Ingredients:

UK: 200g canned chickpeas (drained and mashed), 1 tablespoon vegan mayo, 1 teaspoon Dijon mustard, 1 tablespoon capers, salt and pepper to taste, 4 large wraps, 50g lettuce

US: 7 oz canned chickpeas, 1 tablespoon vegan mayo, 1 teaspoon Dijon mustard, 1 tablespoon capers, salt and pepper, 4 large wraps, 1.8 oz lettuce

Instructions:

1. In a bowl, combine mashed chickpeas, vegan mayo, mustard, capers, salt, and pepper.
2. Spread the mixture over each wrap and top with lettuce.
3. Wrap it up and enjoy a refreshing, plant-based lunch!

Nutrition Info (per wrap): Calories: 310 | Fat: 9g | Carbs: 42g | Protein: 12g

GREEK-STYLE VEGGIE WRAP

Prep: 10 mins | **Cook:** 0 mins | **Serves:** 2
Cooking Function: None
Ingredients:

UK: 100g feta cheese (crumbled), 1 cucumber (sliced), 1 tomato (diced), 1 red onion (sliced), 4 large wraps, 50g tzatziki

US: 3.5 oz feta cheese, 1 cucumber, 1 tomato, 1 red onion, 4 large wraps, 1.8 oz tzatziki

Instructions:

1. Spread tzatziki on each wrap.
2. Layer with cucumber, tomato, onion, and crumbled feta.
3. Wrap it up and relish this refreshing Mediterranean meal!

Nutrition Info (per wrap): Calories: 350 | Fat: 20g | Carbs: 30g | Protein: 12g

TOFU SCRAMBLE BREAKFAST WRAP

Prep: 10 mins | **Cook:** 10 mins | **Serves:** 2
Cooking Function: Cook
Ingredients:

UK: 200g firm tofu (crumbled), 1 teaspoon turmeric, 1 tablespoon nutritional yeast, 1 tablespoon olive oil, salt and pepper, 4 large wraps, mixed salad leaves

US: 7 oz firm tofu, 1 teaspoon turmeric, 1 tablespoon nutritional yeast, 1 tablespoon olive oil, salt and pepper, 4 large wraps, mixed salad leaves

Instructions:

1. In a pan, heat olive oil and add crumbled tofu, turmeric, nutritional yeast, salt, and pepper. Cook for about 5-7 minutes until heated through.
2. Warm the wraps in the microwave for a few seconds.
3. Spread the tofu scramble over each wrap, top with mixed salad leaves, and wrap tightly.
4. Enjoy this hearty breakfast wrap any time of day!

Nutrition Info (per wrap): Calories: 340 | Fat: 18g | Carbs: 25g | Protein: 20g

LENTIL AND SPINACH CURRY WRAP

Prep: 10 mins | **Cook:** 30 mins | **Serves:** 2
Cooking Function: Cook
Ingredients:

UK: 200g canned lentils (drained), 100g spinach, 1 tablespoon curry paste, 2 large wraps, 50g yogurt (optional)

US: 7 oz canned lentils, 3.5 oz spinach, 1 tablespoon curry paste, 2 large wraps, 1.8 oz yoghurt

Instructions:

1. In a pan, cook lentils and curry paste over medium heat for about 10 minutes.
2. Add spinach and cook until wilted.
3. Spread the mixture over each wrap and drizzle with yoghurt if desired.
4. Wrap it up and indulge in this flavourful meal!

Nutrition Info (per wrap): Calories: 380 | Fat: 10g | Carbs: 56g | Protein: 20g

CAPRESE WRAP WITH BALSAMIC GLAZE

Prep: 10 mins | **Cook:** 0 mins | **Serves:** 2

Cooking Function: None

Ingredients:

UK: 100g mozzarella (sliced), 1 tomato (sliced), fresh basil leaves, 2 large wraps, 30ml balsamic glaze

US: 3.5 oz mozzarella, 1 tomato, fresh basil leaves, 2 large wraps, 1 ounce balsamic glaze

Instructions:

1. Spread mozzarella and tomato slices over each wrap.
2. Top with fresh basil and drizzle with balsamic glaze.
3. Wrap it up and enjoy this fresh, Italian-inspired meal!

Nutrition Info (per wrap): Calories: 320 | Fat: 18g | Carbs: 30g | Protein: 15g

VEGAN 'FISH' FINGER WRAP

Prep: 15 mins | **Cook:** 20 mins | **Serves:** 2
Cooking Function: Air Fry
Ingredients:
UK: 200g vegan fish fingers, 4 large wraps, 100g tartar sauce, mixed salad leaves
US: 7 oz vegan fish fingers, 4 large wraps, 3.5 oz tartar sauce, mixed salad leaves
Instructions:
1. Preheat the air fryer to 200°C (400°F).
2. Cook vegan fish fingers for about 15 minutes until golden.
3. Spread tartar sauce on each wrap, add salad leaves, and top with fish fingers.
4. Wrap it up and enjoy this fun, nostalgic meal!

Nutrition Info (per wrap): Calories: 420 | Fat: 22g | Carbs: 38g | Protein: 12g

CHAPTER 5: GLOBAL FLAVOURS

MEXICAN STREET CORN WRAP

Prep: 10 mins | Cook: 15 mins | Serves: 2
Cooking Function: Air Fry
Ingredients:

UK: 200g corn (canned or frozen), 30ml mayonnaise, 30g feta cheese (crumbled), 1 teaspoon chilli powder, 2 large wraps, fresh cilantro (for garnish)

US: 7 oz corn, 1 oz mayonnaise, 1 oz feta cheese, 1 teaspoon chilli powder, 2 large wraps, fresh cilantro

Instructions:

1. Preheat your air fryer to 200°C (400°F).
2. If using frozen corn, thaw it in the microwave for a few minutes.
3. In a bowl, mix corn, mayonnaise, feta, chilli powder, salt, and pepper.
4. Spread the mixture evenly over the large wraps.
5. Roll them tightly, and place them in the air fryer basket.
6. Cook for about 8-10 minutes, until the wraps are golden and crispy.
7. Once cooked, remove from the air fryer, garnish with fresh cilantro, and serve hot!

Nutrition Info (per wrap): Calories: 340 | Fat: 16g | Carbs: 36g | Protein: 10g

JAPANESE TERIYAKI CHICKEN WRAP

Prep: 10 mins | Cook: 15 mins | Serves: 2
Cooking Function: Cook
Ingredients:

UK: 200g chicken breast (cooked and sliced), 30ml teriyaki sauce, 1 carrot (julienned), 50g cucumber (sliced), 2 large wraps, sesame seeds (for garnish)

US: 7 oz chicken breast, 1 oz teriyaki sauce, 1 carrot, 1.8 oz cucumber, 2 large wraps, sesame seeds

Instructions:

1. In a bowl, toss the sliced chicken with teriyaki sauce until well coated.
2. Warm the large wraps in the microwave for a few seconds.
3. Spread the chicken mixture on each wrap and add carrot and cucumber.
4. Roll tightly and cut in half.
5. Sprinkle with sesame seeds before serving. Enjoy this delightful wrap!

Nutrition Info (per wrap): Calories: 420 | Fat: 9g | Carbs: 32g | Protein: 38g

INDIAN BUTTER CHICKEN WRAP

Prep: 10 mins | **Cook:** 20 mins | **Serves:** 2
Cooking Function: Air Fry
Ingredients:
UK: 200g cooked chicken (diced), 50ml butter chicken sauce, 2 large wraps, 50g spinach, 30g yogurt (optional)
US: 7 oz cooked chicken, 1.7 oz butter chicken sauce, 2 large wraps, 1.8 oz spinach, 1 oz yogurt
Instructions:
1. Preheat your air fryer to 180°C (360°F).
2. In a bowl, mix the diced chicken with butter chicken sauce.
3. Lay the wraps flat and add spinach and the chicken mixture.
4. Roll up the wraps tightly and place them in the air fryer basket.
5. Cook for about 10-12 minutes, until golden brown.
6. If desired, serve with a dollop of yoghurt for extra creaminess.

Nutrition Info (per wrap): Calories: 460 | Fat: 15g | Carbs: 38g | Protein: 30g

VIETNAMESE BANH MI WRAP

Prep: 10 mins | **Cook:** 0 mins | **Serves:** 2
Cooking Function: None
Ingredients:
UK: 100g cooked pork (sliced), 30g pickled carrots, 30g cucumber (sliced), fresh coriander, 2 large wraps, 30ml mayonnaise
US: 3.5 oz cooked pork, 1 oz pickled carrots, 1 oz cucumber, fresh coriander, 2 large wraps, 1 oz mayonnaise
Instructions:
1. Spread mayonnaise on each wrap.
2. Layer with sliced pork, pickled carrots, cucumber, and fresh coriander.
3. Roll tightly and enjoy this fresh and vibrant wrap!

Nutrition Info (per wrap): Calories: 350 | Fat: 14g | Carbs: 32g | Protein: 20g

GREEK GYROS WRAP

Prep: 10 mins | **Cook:** 0 mins | **Serves:** 2
Cooking Function: None
Ingredients:
UK: 200g cooked lamb (sliced), 50g tzatziki, 1 tomato (sliced), 50g lettuce, 2 large wraps
US: 7 oz cooked lamb, 1.8 oz tzatziki, 1 tomato, 1.8 oz lettuce, 2 large wraps
Instructions:
1. Spread tzatziki over each wrap.
2. Add sliced lamb, tomato, and lettuce.
3. Roll up and enjoy this delicious Mediterranean favourite!

Nutrition Info (per wrap): Calories: 480 | Fat: 22g | Carbs: 38g | Protein: 35g

KOREAN BBQ BEEF WRAP

Prep: 15 mins | **Cook:** 15 mins | **Serves:** 2
Cooking Function: Air Fry
Ingredients:
UK: 200g beef (marinated in soy sauce), 50g kimchi, 2 large wraps, 50g cucumber (sliced), sesame seeds (for garnish)
US: 7 oz beef, 1.8 oz kimchi, 2 large wraps, 1.8 oz cucumber, sesame seeds
Instructions:
1. Preheat your air fryer to 200°C (400°F).
2. Cook marinated beef for about 10-12 minutes until done.
3. Lay the wraps flat and add cooked beef, kimchi, and cucumber.
4. Roll tightly and sprinkle with sesame seeds before serving.

Nutrition Info (per wrap): Calories: 550 | Fat: 27g | Carbs: 42g | Protein: 36g

ITALIAN CAPRESE WRAP

Prep: 10 mins | **Cook:** 0 mins | **Serves:** 2
Cooking Function: None
Ingredients:
UK: 100g mozzarella (sliced), 1 tomato (sliced), fresh basil leaves, 2 large wraps, 30ml balsamic glaze
US: 3.5 oz mozzarella, 1 tomato, fresh basil leaves, 2 large wraps, 1 oz balsamic glaze
Instructions:
1. Spread mozzarella and tomato slices over each wrap.
2. Top with fresh basil and drizzle with balsamic glaze.
3. Roll it up and enjoy this fresh and classic Italian dish!

Nutrition Info (per wrap): Calories: 320 | Fat: 18g | Carbs: 30g | Protein: 15g

THAI GREEN CURRY WRAP

Prep: 10 mins | **Cook:** 20 mins | **Serves:** 2
Cooking Function: Air Fry
Ingredients:
UK: 200g cooked chicken (diced), 30ml green curry paste, 50g spinach, 2 large wraps, 30g coconut cream
US: 7 oz cooked chicken, 1 oz green curry paste, 1.8 oz spinach, 2 large wraps, 1 oz coconut cream
Instructions:
1. In a pan, heat curry paste with coconut cream and stir in the chicken.
2. Add spinach until wilted, about 2-3 minutes.
3. Warm the wraps in the microwave for a few seconds.
4. Spread the mixture evenly over the wraps and roll tightly.
5. Serve warm and savour the delightful Thai flavours!

Nutrition Info (per wrap): Calories: 450 | Fat: 20g | Carbs: 30g | Protein: 30g

AMERICAN PHILLY CHEESESTEAK WRAP

Prep: 10 mins | **Cook:** 15 mins | **Serves:** 2
Cooking Function: Cook
Ingredients:
UK: 200g steak (sliced), 50g bell peppers (sliced), 50g onions (sliced), 50g cheese (sliced), 2 large wraps
US: 7 oz steak, 1.8 oz bell peppers, 1.8 oz onions, 1.8 oz cheese, 2 large wraps
Instructions:
1. In a pan, sauté onions and bell peppers until soft.
2. Add the sliced steak and cook for about 5 minutes until done.
3. Lay the mixture on each wrap and top with cheese.
4. Roll up tightly and serve hot for a true Philly experience!

Nutrition Info (per wrap): Calories: 560 | Fat: 32g | Carbs: 38g | Protein: 40g

MIDDLE EASTERN SHAWARMA WRAP

Prep: 10 mins | **Cook:** 15 mins | **Serves:** 2
Cooking Function: Air Fry
Ingredients:
UK: 200g chicken (marinated in shawarma spices), 50g tahini, 50g lettuce, 2 large wraps, 1 tomato (sliced)
US: 7 oz chicken, 1.8 oz tahini, 1.8 oz lettuce, 2 large wraps, 1 tomato
Instructions:
1. Preheat your air fryer to 200°C (400°F).
2. Cook marinated chicken for about 10-12 minutes until fully cooked.
3. Lay the wraps flat, spread tahini, and add cooked chicken, lettuce, and tomato.
4. Roll tightly and serve hot for a taste of the Middle East!

Nutrition Info (per wrap): Calories: 480 | Fat: 22g | Carbs: 40g | Protein: 36g

SPANISH TORTILLA WRAP

Prep: 10 mins | **Cook:** 15 mins | **Serves:** 2
Cooking Function: Cook
Ingredients:

UK: 200g potatoes (cooked and sliced), 50g onion (sautéed), 2 large wraps, 3 eggs (beaten), salt, and pepper

US: 7 oz potatoes, 1.8 oz onion, 2 large wraps, 3 eggs

Instructions:

1. In a bowl, mix cooked potatoes, sautéed onion, and beaten eggs.
2. Heat a non-stick pan, pour the mixture, and cook until set.
3. Warm the wraps and fill them with the tortilla mixture.
4. Roll and serve warm for a comforting Spanish delight!

Nutrition Info (per wrap): Calories: 450 | Fat: 20g | Carbs: 40g | Protein: 20g

RUSSIAN BEEF STROGANOFF WRAP

Prep: 10 mins | Cook: 20 mins | Serves: 2
Cooking Function: Cook
Ingredients:

UK: 200g beef (sliced), 100g mushrooms (sliced), 50ml sour cream, 2 large wraps, 50g onions (sautéed)

US: 7 oz beef, 3.5 oz mushrooms, 1.7 oz sour cream, 2 large wraps, 1.8 oz onions

Instructions:

1. In a pan, cook onions and mushrooms until soft.
2. Add beef and cook until browned.
3. Stir in sour cream and cook for another 2-3 minutes.
4. Lay the mixture on the wraps and roll tightly. Serve hot for a creamy experience!

Nutrition Info (per wrap): Calories: 550 | Fat: 28g | Carbs: 32g | Protein: 36g

JAMAICAN JERK CHICKEN WRAP

Prep: 10 mins | **Cook:** 15 mins | **Serves:** 2
Cooking Function: Air Fry
Ingredients:
UK: 200g chicken (marinated in jerk seasoning), 50g mango salsa, 2 large wraps, 50g lettuce
US: 7 oz chicken, 1.8 oz mango salsa, 2 large wraps, 1.8 oz lettuce
Instructions:
1. Preheat your air fryer to 200°C (400°F).
2. Cook marinated chicken for about 10-12 minutes until done.
3. Lay the wraps flat, add lettuce, and cooked chicken, and top with mango salsa.
4. Roll tightly and serve hot for a taste of the Caribbean!

Nutrition Info (per wrap): Calories: 480 | Fat: 20g | Carbs: 38g | Protein: 36g

CHAPTER 6: HEALTHY AND LIGHT

QUINOA AND ROASTED VEGETABLE WRAP

Prep: 10 mins | **Cook:** 30 mins | **Serves:** 2
Cooking Function: Roast
Ingredients:

UK: 100g quinoa (rinsed), 200g mixed vegetables (e.g., bell peppers, zucchini, and red onion, chopped), 15ml olive oil, 1 teaspoon paprika, salt, pepper, 2 large wholemeal wraps

US: 3.5 oz quinoa, 7 oz mixed vegetables, 0.5 oz olive oil, 1 teaspoon paprika, salt, pepper, 2 large wholemeal wraps

Instructions:

1. Preheat your oven to 200°C (400°F) for roasting the veggies.
2. Toss the mixed vegetables with olive oil, paprika, salt, and pepper in a bowl.
3. Spread the vegetables on a baking tray and roast for about 20 minutes until tender.
4. While the veggies roast, cook quinoa according to package instructions until fluffy (around 15 minutes).
5. Once cooked, combine quinoa with roasted vegetables.
6. Lay the mixture in the centre of each wrap, fold the sides, and roll tightly.
7. Serve warm for a nutritious, filling meal!

Nutrition Info (per wrap): Calories: 350 | Fat: 8g | Carbs: 60g | Protein: 12g

GRILLED CHICKEN AND AVOCADO LETTUCE WRAP

Prep: 10 mins | **Cook:** 15 mins | **Serves:** 2
Cooking Function: Grill
Ingredients:

UK: 200g chicken breast (grilled and sliced), 1 ripe avocado (sliced), 4 large lettuce leaves, 30g cherry tomatoes (halved), 15ml lime juice, salt, pepper

US: 7 oz chicken breast, 1 avocado, 4 large lettuce leaves, 1 oz cherry tomatoes, 0.5 oz lime juice, salt, pepper

Instructions:
1. Grill the chicken breast on medium heat for about 5-7 minutes per side until fully cooked.
2. Slice the grilled chicken and set aside.
3. In a bowl, toss cherry tomatoes with lime juice, salt, and pepper.
4. Lay a lettuce leaf flat, and fill with chicken, avocado, and tomato mix.
5. Roll the lettuce to form a wrap.
6. Enjoy fresh for a light and healthy lunch!

Nutrition Info (per wrap): Calories: 320 | Fat: 15g | Carbs: 12g | Protein: 30g

SMOKED SALMON AND CUCUMBER ROLL

Prep: 5 mins | **Cook:** 0 mins | **Serves:** 2
Cooking Function: None

Ingredients:
UK: 150g smoked salmon, 1 medium cucumber (thinly sliced), 100g cream cheese, 2 large wholemeal wraps, dill (for garnish)
US: 5.3 oz smoked salmon, 1 cucumber, 3.5 oz cream cheese, 2 large wholemeal wraps, dill

Instructions:
1. Spread cream cheese evenly over each wrap.
2. Layer smoked salmon and cucumber slices on top.
3. Roll tightly and slice into bite-sized pieces.
4. Garnish with dill before serving for a refreshing snack!

Nutrition Info (per roll): Calories: 250 | Fat: 15g | Carbs: 20g | Protein: 15g

TURKEY AND HUMMUS PINWHEELS

Prep: 10 mins | **Cook:** 0 mins | **Serves:** 2
Cooking Function: None
Ingredients:
UK: 100g sliced turkey breast, 50g hummus, 2 large wraps, 30g spinach, 15g grated carrot
US: 3.5 oz sliced turkey breast, 1.8 oz hummus, 2 large wraps, 1 oz spinach, 0.5 oz grated carrot
Instructions:
1. Spread hummus on each wrap, covering evenly.
2. Layer turkey, spinach, and grated carrot on top.
3. Roll the wraps tightly and slice into pinwheels.
4. Enjoy as a healthy, protein-packed snack!

Nutrition Info (per pinwheel): Calories: 220 | Fat: 5g | Carbs: 22g | Protein: 18g

TABBOULEH AND FETA WRAP

Prep: 10 mins | **Cook:** 0 mins | **Serves:** 2
Cooking Function: None
Ingredients:
UK: 100g bulgur wheat (cooked), 50g parsley (finely chopped), 30g feta cheese (crumbled), 2 large wraps, 1 medium tomato (diced), 15ml olive oil, lemon juice, salt, pepper
US: 3.5 oz bulgur wheat, 1.8 oz parsley, 1 oz feta cheese, 2 large wraps, 1 tomato, 0.5 oz olive oil, lemon juice, salt, pepper
Instructions:
1. In a bowl, mix cooked bulgur, parsley, feta, diced tomato, olive oil, lemon juice, salt, and pepper.
2. Spoon the mixture onto each wrap.
3. Roll tightly and slice in half.
4. Serve fresh for a delicious Mediterranean treat!

Nutrition Info (per wrap): Calories: 300 | Fat: 12g | Carbs: 36g | Protein: 10g

TOFU AND VEGETABLE SPRING ROLLS

Prep: 15 mins | **Cook:** 15 mins | **Serves:** 2
Cooking Function: Fry
Ingredients:
UK: 200g firm tofu (sliced), 100g mixed vegetables (e.g., carrots, bell peppers, and bean sprouts), 2 large rice paper wraps, 15ml soy sauce, 10ml sesame oil
US: 7 oz firm tofu, 3.5 oz mixed vegetables, 2 large rice paper wraps, 0.5 oz soy sauce, 0.3 oz sesame oil
Instructions:
1. Heat sesame oil in a pan and stir-fry tofu and vegetables for about 5-7 minutes.
2. In a bowl, dip rice paper wraps in warm water until soft.
3. Place the tofu and vegetable mixture in the centre of each wrap.
4. Fold in the sides and roll tightly.
5. Serve with soy sauce for dipping.
Nutrition Info (per roll): Calories: 220 | Fat: 10g | Carbs: 24g | Protein: 14g

EGG WHITE AND SPINACH BREAKFAST WRAP

Prep: 5 mins | **Cook:** 10 mins | **Serves:** 2
Cooking Function: Fry
Ingredients:
UK: 4 egg whites, 50g spinach, 2 large wraps, 15ml olive oil, salt, pepper
US: 4 egg whites, 1.8 oz spinach, 2 large wraps, 0.5 oz olive oil, salt, pepper
Instructions:
1. In a pan, heat olive oil over medium heat.
2. Add spinach and cook until wilted (about 2 minutes).
3. Pour in egg whites, season with salt and pepper, and cook until set.
4. Spoon the mixture onto wraps, roll tightly, and enjoy a healthy breakfast!
Nutrition Info (per wrap): Calories: 200 | Fat: 8g | Carbs: 20g | Protein: 14g

LENTIL AND SWEET POTATO WRAP

Prep: 10 mins | Cook: 20 mins | Serves: 2
Cooking Function: Bake
Ingredients:

UK: 150g sweet potato (peeled and diced), 100g cooked lentils, 2 large wraps, 15ml olive oil, salt, pepper, 1 teaspoon cumin

US: 5.3 oz sweet potato, 3.5 oz cooked lentils, 2 large wraps, 0.5 oz olive oil, salt, pepper, 1 teaspoon cumin

Instructions:

1. Preheat your oven to 200°C (400°F) for baking sweet potatoes.
2. Toss diced sweet potatoes with olive oil, cumin, salt, and pepper, then spread on a baking tray.
3. Bake for 15 minutes until tender.
4. Combine baked sweet potatoes with lentils.
5. Fill each wrap with the mixture and roll tightly.
6. Serve warm for a wholesome meal!

Nutrition Info (per wrap): Calories: 320 | Fat: 9g | Carbs: 54g | Protein: 10g

TUNA NICOISE SALAD WRAP

Prep: 10 mins | Cook: 0 mins | Serves: 2
Cooking Function: None
Ingredients:

UK: 200g canned tuna (drained), 50g green beans (blanched), 2 hard-boiled eggs (sliced), 30g olives, 2 large wraps, 15ml vinaigrette

US: 7 oz canned tuna, 1.8 oz green beans, 2 hard-boiled eggs, 1 oz olives, 2 large wraps, 0.5 oz vinaigrette

Instructions:

1. In a bowl, mix tuna, green beans, olives, and vinaigrette.
2. Lay the mixture and sliced eggs in the centre of each wrap.
3. Roll tightly and slice in half for a filling lunch!

Nutrition Info (per wrap): Calories: 350 | Fat: 15g | Carbs: 20g | Protein: 28g

CAULIFLOWER RICE AND BLACK BEAN BURRITO

Prep: 10 mins | **Cook:** 15 mins | **Serves:** 2

Cooking Function: Steam Bake

Ingredients:

UK: 200g cauliflower rice, 100g black beans (drained), 50g corn, 2 large wraps, 15ml salsa, 10g fresh coriander (chopped)

US: 7 oz cauliflower rice, 3.5 oz black beans, 1.8 oz corn, 2 large wraps, 0.5 oz salsa, 0.4 oz fresh coriander

Instructions:

1. Steam cauliflower rice until tender (about 5 minutes).
2. In a bowl, mix steamed cauliflower rice, black beans, corn, and salsa.
3. Spoon the mixture onto wraps, sprinkle with coriander, and roll tightly.
4. Serve warm for a nutritious, delicious burrito!

Nutrition Info (per burrito): Calories: 300 | Fat: 8g | Carbs: 50g | Protein: 12g

GRILLED PRAWN AND MANGO WRAP

Prep: 10 mins | **Cook:** 10 mins | **Serves:** 2

Cooking Function: Grill

Ingredients:

UK: 200g prawns (peeled and deveined), 1 ripe mango (sliced), 2 large wraps, 15ml lime juice, salt, pepper, 30g mixed salad leaves

US: 7 oz prawns, 1 mango, 2 large wraps, 0.5 oz lime juice, salt, pepper, 1 oz mixed salad leaves

Instructions:

1. Preheat the grill to medium-high heat.
2. Toss prawns with lime juice, salt, and pepper.
3. Grill prawns for about 2-3 minutes on each side until pink.
4. Lay grilled prawns and mango on wraps with salad leaves.
5. Roll tightly and serve for a fruity, fresh meal!

Nutrition Info (per wrap): Calories: 320 | Fat: 7g | Carbs: 40g | Protein: 20g

ZUCCHINI NOODLE AND PESTO WRAP

Prep: 10 mins | Cook: 5 mins | Serves: 2
Cooking Function: Sauté
Ingredients:

UK: 200g zucchini (spiralized), 30g pesto, 2 large wraps, 15ml olive oil, 10g pine nuts (toasted), salt, pepper

US: 7 oz zucchini, 1 oz pesto, 2 large wraps, 0.5 oz olive oil, 0.4 oz pine nuts, salt, pepper

Instructions:

1. In a pan, heat olive oil over medium heat and sauté zucchini noodles for about 3-5 minutes.
2. Stir in pesto, salt, and pepper until well combined.
3. Fill wraps with the zucchini mixture and sprinkle with toasted pine nuts.
4. Roll tightly and enjoy a low-carb, flavorful meal!

Nutrition Info (per wrap): Calories: 280 | Fat: 15g | Carbs: 30g | Protein: 8g

BEETROOT HUMMUS AND GOAT CHEESE WRAP

Prep: 10 mins | Cook: 0 mins | Serves: 2
Cooking Function: None
Ingredients:

UK: 100g beetroot hummus, 50g goat cheese (crumbled), 2 large wraps, 30g rocket leaves, 15ml balsamic glaze

US: 3.5 oz beetroot hummus, 1.8 oz goat cheese, 2 large wraps, 1 oz rocket leaves, 0.5 oz balsamic glaze

Instructions:

1. Spread beetroot hummus evenly over each wrap.
2. Top with crumbled goat cheese and rocket leaves.
3. Drizzle with balsamic glaze before rolling tightly.
4. Slice in half and serve for a vibrant, tasty lunch!

Nutrition Info (per wrap): Calories: 300 | Fat: 15g | Carbs: 36g | Protein: 10g

CHAPTER 7: PARTY AND PICNIC WRAPS

MINI WRAP PINWHEELS PLATTER

Prep: 15 mins | **Cook:** 0 mins | **Serves:** 4
Cooking Function: None
Ingredients:

UK: 4 large wraps, 100g cream cheese, 50g sliced ham, 50g sliced turkey, 50g grated cheese, 50g cucumber (thinly sliced), 50g bell pepper (thinly sliced), salt, pepper

US: 4 large wraps, 3.5 oz cream cheese, 1.8 oz sliced ham, 1.8 oz sliced turkey, 1.8 oz grated cheese, 1.8 oz cucumber, 1.8 oz bell pepper, salt, pepper

Instructions:

1. Spread a layer of cream cheese evenly on each wrap.
2. Lay the sliced ham, turkey, grated cheese, cucumber, and bell pepper on top.
3. Season with salt and pepper.
4. Starting from one end, tightly roll up each wrap.
5. Slice into pinwheels and arrange on a platter.
6. Serve chilled or at room temperature for a delightful party snack!

Nutrition Info (per serving): Calories: 210 | Fat: 12g | Carbs: 18g | Protein: 10g

CLUB SANDWICH WRAP

Prep: 10 mins | **Cook:** 0 mins | **Serves:** 2
Cooking Function: None
Ingredients:

UK: 2 large wraps, 100g cooked chicken (sliced), 50g bacon (cooked and crumbled), 50g lettuce, 50g tomato (sliced), 30ml mayonnaise, salt, pepper

US: 2 large wraps, 3.5 oz cooked chicken, 1.8 oz bacon, 1.8 oz lettuce, 1.8 oz tomato, 1 oz mayonnaise, salt, pepper

Instructions:

1. Spread mayonnaise evenly over each wrap.
2. Layer sliced chicken, crumbled bacon, lettuce, and tomato on top.
3. Season with salt and pepper.
4. Roll up tightly from one end to the other.
5. Slice in half and serve for a hearty lunch option!

Nutrition Info (per serving): Calories: 400 | Fat: 20g | Carbs: 30g | Protein: 30g

ANTIPASTI WRAP SKEWERS

Prep: 15 mins | **Cook:** 0 mins | **Serves:** 4
Cooking Function: None
Ingredients:

UK: 4 large wraps, 100g salami (sliced), 100g mozzarella balls, 100g cherry tomatoes, 50g olives, 50g roasted red peppers, 15ml balsamic glaze

US: 4 large wraps, 3.5 oz salami, 3.5 oz mozzarella balls, 3.5 oz cherry tomatoes, 1.8 oz olives, 1.8 oz roasted red peppers, 0.5 oz balsamic glaze

Instructions:

1. Lay a large wrap flat and layer with salami, mozzarella, cherry tomatoes, olives, and roasted peppers.
2. Roll the wrap tightly and cut into bite-sized pieces.
3. Thread each piece onto skewers, alternating with cherry tomatoes.
4. Drizzle with balsamic glaze before serving.
5. Enjoy as a fun appetizer!

Nutrition Info (per serving): Calories: 220 | Fat: 15g | Carbs: 8g | Protein: 12g

CHICKEN AND STUFFING WRAP ROLLS

Prep: 10 mins | **Cook:** 15 mins | **Serves:** 2
Cooking Function: Bake
Ingredients:

UK: 2 large wraps, 200g cooked chicken (shredded), 100g stuffing mix, 100ml chicken broth, 30ml cranberry sauce

US: 2 large wraps, 7 oz cooked chicken, 3.5 oz stuffing mix, 3.4 oz chicken broth, 1 oz cranberry sauce

Instructions:

1. Preheat your oven to 180°C (350°F).
2. In a bowl, mix shredded chicken with stuffing mix and chicken broth until well combined.
3. Spread the mixture evenly over each wrap.
4. Roll tightly and place in a baking dish.
5. Bake for about 10-15 minutes until heated through.
6. Serve with cranberry sauce for dipping!

Nutrition Info (per serving): Calories: 350 | Fat: 9g | Carbs: 30g | Protein: 40g

SMOKED SALMON AND CREAM CHEESE SPIRALS

Prep: 10 mins | **Cook:** 0 mins | **Serves:** 4

Cooking Function: None

Ingredients:

UK: 4 large wraps, 100g cream cheese, 100g smoked salmon, 50g capers, 50g arugula, lemon wedges (for serving)

US: 4 large wraps, 3.5 oz cream cheese, 3.5 oz smoked salmon, 1.8 oz capers, 1.8 oz arugula, lemon wedges

Instructions:

1. Spread cream cheese evenly over each wrap.
2. Lay smoked salmon, capers, and arugula on top.
3. Roll tightly and slice into spirals.
4. Serve with lemon wedges for a zesty touch!

Nutrition Info (per serving): Calories: 280 | Fat: 15g | Carbs: 20g | Protein: 18g

VEGETABLE CRUDITÉ HUMMUS WRAPS

Prep: 15 mins | **Cook:** 0 mins | **Serves:** 2

Cooking Function: None

Ingredients:

UK: 2 large wraps, 150g hummus, 50g carrot sticks, 50g cucumber sticks, 50g bell pepper strips, salt, pepper

US: 2 large wraps, 5.3 oz hummus, 1.8 oz carrot sticks, 1.8 oz cucumber sticks, 1.8 oz bell pepper strips, salt, pepper

Instructions:

1. Spread hummus evenly on each wrap.
2. Lay the vegetable sticks on top.
3. Season with salt and pepper.
4. Roll tightly and slice in half for a refreshing snack!

Nutrition Info (per serving): Calories: 250 | Fat: 10g | Carbs: 30g | Protein: 8g

CORONATION CHICKEN VOL-AU-WRAP

Prep: 10 mins | Cook: 0 mins | Serves: 4
Cooking Function: None
Ingredients:

UK: 4 large wraps, 200g cooked chicken (shredded), 50ml mayonnaise, 15ml curry powder, 50g raisins, 50g lettuce

US: 4 large wraps, 7 oz cooked chicken, 1.8 oz mayonnaise, 0.5 oz curry powder, 1.8 oz raisins, 1.8 oz lettuce

Instructions:

1. In a bowl, mix shredded chicken with mayonnaise, curry powder, and raisins.
2. Spread the mixture evenly over each wrap.
3. Top with lettuce and roll tightly.
4. Slice in half and enjoy a taste of the tropics!

Nutrition Info (per serving): Calories: 330 | Fat: 15g | Carbs: 30g | Protein: 25g

PESTO AND SUN-DRIED TOMATO PINWHEELS

Prep: 10 mins | Cook: 0 mins | Serves: 4
Cooking Function: None
Ingredients:

UK: 4 large wraps, 100g pesto, 100g sun-dried tomatoes (drained), 50g feta cheese (crumbled), 50g spinach

US: 4 large wraps, 3.5 oz pesto, 3.5 oz sun-dried tomatoes, 1.8 oz feta cheese, 1.8 oz spinach

Instructions:

1. Spread pesto evenly over each wrap.
2. Top with sun-dried tomatoes, crumbled feta, and spinach.
3. Roll tightly and slice into pinwheels.
4. Serve as a vibrant appetizer!

Nutrition Info (per serving): Calories: 290 | Fat: 20g | Carbs: 22g | Protein: 8g

HAM AND CHEESE WRAP STRAWS

Prep: 10 mins | **Cook:** 10 mins | **Serves:** 4
Cooking Function: Bake
Ingredients:
UK: 4 large wraps, 100g ham (sliced), 100g cheese (sliced), 15ml mustard, 15ml olive oil
US: 4 large wraps, 3.5 oz ham, 3.5 oz cheese, 0.5 oz mustard, 0.5 oz olive oil
Instructions:
1. Preheat your oven to 200°C (400°F).
2. Spread mustard evenly on each wrap.
3. Layer ham and cheese on top.
4. Roll up tightly and slice into straws.
5. Brush with olive oil and bake for about 10 minutes until golden.
6. Serve warm for a cheesy treat!

Nutrition Info (per serving): Calories: 350 | Fat: 20g | Carbs: 30g | Protein: 18g

EGG AND WATERCRESS FINGER WRAPS

Prep: 10 mins | **Cook:** 10 mins | **Serves:** 4
Cooking Function: None
Ingredients:
UK: 4 large wraps, 4 boiled eggs (chopped), 50g watercress, 30ml mayonnaise, salt, pepper
US: 4 large wraps, 4 boiled eggs, 1.8 oz watercress, 1 oz mayonnaise, salt, pepper
Instructions:
1. In a bowl, mix chopped eggs with mayonnaise, salt, and pepper.
2. Spread the egg mixture evenly on each wrap.
3. Top with watercress and roll tightly.
4. Cut into finger-sized pieces for easy serving!

Nutrition Info (per serving): Calories: 220 | Fat: 12g | Carbs: 15g | Protein: 14g

ROAST BEEF AND HORSERADISH SPIRALS

Prep: 10 mins | **Cook:** 0 mins | **Serves:** 4

Cooking Function: None

Ingredients:

UK: 4 large wraps, 100g roast beef (sliced), 30ml horseradish sauce, 50g lettuce, 50g cucumber (sliced)

US: 4 large wraps, 3.5 oz roast beef, 1 oz horseradish sauce, 1.8 oz lettuce, 1.8 oz cucumber

Instructions:

1. Spread horseradish sauce over each wrap.
2. Layer with roast beef, lettuce, and cucumber.
3. Roll tightly and slice into spirals.
4. Serve for a punchy snack!

Nutrition Info (per serving): Calories: 320 | Fat: 14g | Carbs: 24g | Protein: 28g

VEGAN RAINBOW VEGGIE WRAP BITES

Prep: 15 mins | Cook: 0 mins | Serves: 4
Cooking Function: None
Ingredients:

UK: 4 large wraps, 100g hummus, 50g red cabbage (shredded), 50g carrots (grated), 50g cucumber (sliced), 50g bell pepper (sliced), 50g avocado (sliced)

US: 4 large wraps, 3.5 oz hummus, 1.8 oz red cabbage, 1.8 oz carrots, 1.8 oz cucumber, 1.8 oz bell pepper, 1.8 oz avocado

Instructions:

1. Spread hummus evenly on each wrap.
2. Layer with shredded cabbage, grated carrots, cucumber, bell pepper, and avocado.
3. Roll tightly and slice into bite-sized pieces.
4. Enjoy a burst of colour and nutrition!

Nutrition Info (per serving): Calories: 200 | Fat: 10g | Carbs: 26g | Protein: 5g

PRAWN COCKTAIL LETTUCE CUPS

Prep: 10 mins | Cook: 0 mins | Serves: 4
Cooking Function: None
Ingredients:

UK: 8 lettuce leaves, 200g cooked prawns, 50g cocktail sauce, 50g cucumber (diced), 50g avocado (diced)

US: 8 lettuce leaves, 7 oz cooked prawns, 1.8 oz cocktail sauce, 1.8 oz cucumber, 1.8 oz avocado

Instructions:

1. In a bowl, mix cooked prawns with cocktail sauce, cucumber, and avocado.
2. Spoon the mixture into lettuce leaves.
3. Serve immediately for a fresh and elegant appetizer!

Nutrition Info (per serving): Calories: 150 | Fat: 5g | Carbs: 10g | Protein: 20g

CHAPTER 8: SWEET TREATS AND DESSERT WRAPS

BANANA AND NUTELLA CREPE

Prep: 10 mins | **Cook:** 15 mins | **Serves:** 2
Cooking Function: None
Ingredients:
UK: 2 large crepes, 2 bananas (sliced), 60g Nutella, 30ml double cream (whipped), icing sugar (for dusting)
US: 2 large crepes, 2 bananas, 2 oz Nutella, 1 oz double cream, icing sugar
Instructions:
1. Spread a generous layer of Nutella on each crepe.
2. Place sliced bananas evenly over the Nutella.
3. Roll the crepes tightly and place them on a serving plate.
4. Drizzle with whipped double cream and dust with icing sugar.
5. Serve immediately for a delightful sweet treat!

Nutrition Info (per serving): Calories: 420 | Fat: 21g | Carbs: 55g | Protein: 6g

APPLE PIE WRAP

Prep: 10 mins | **Cook:** 15 mins | **Serves:** 4
Cooking Function: Air Fry
Ingredients:
UK: 4 large flour tortillas, 300g cooking apples (peeled and diced), 50g sugar, 1 teaspoon cinnamon, 30ml lemon juice, 20g butter (melted)
US: 4 large flour tortillas, 10.6 oz cooking apples, 1.8 oz sugar, 1 teaspoon cinnamon, 1 oz lemon juice, 0.7 oz butter
Instructions:
1. Preheat your air fryer to 180°C (356°F).
2. In a bowl, combine diced apples, sugar, cinnamon, and lemon juice.
3. Lay out the tortillas and fill each with the apple mixture.
4. Roll them up tightly and brush them with melted butter.
5. Place in the air fryer basket and cook for 10-15 minutes until golden and crispy.
6. Let cool slightly, slice, and serve warm!

Nutrition Info (per serving): Calories: 310 | Fat: 9g | Carbs: 54g | Protein: 2g

STRAWBERRIES AND CREAM WRAP

Prep: 10 mins | **Cook:** 0 mins | **Serves:** 2
Cooking Function: None
Ingredients:

UK: 2 large tortillas, 200g strawberries (sliced), 60ml double cream (whipped), 30g icing sugar, mint leaves (for garnish)

US: 2 large tortillas, 7 oz strawberries, 2 oz double cream, 1 oz icing sugar, mint leaves

Instructions:

1. Spread whipped double cream on each tortilla.
2. Layer with sliced strawberries and sprinkle with icing sugar.
3. Roll the tortillas tightly and cut in half.
4. Garnish with mint leaves before serving. Enjoy fresh and fruity!

Nutrition Info (per serving): Calories: 220 | Fat: 9g | Carbs: 31g | Protein: 3g

S'MORES WRAP

Prep: 5 mins | **Cook:** 5 mins | **Serves:** 2
Cooking Function: Air Fry
Ingredients:

UK: 2 large tortillas, 60g milk chocolate (broken into pieces), 50g marshmallows, 30g graham cracker crumbs

US: 2 large tortillas, 2 oz milk chocolate, 1.8 oz marshmallows, 1 oz graham cracker crumbs

Instructions:

1. Preheat your air fryer to 200°C (392°F).
2. Place chocolate pieces and marshmallows on each tortilla.
3. Sprinkle graham cracker crumbs over the top.
4. Roll up the tortillas and place them in the air fryer.
5. Cook for 3-5 minutes until the chocolate is melted and tortillas are golden.
6. Slice and serve immediately for gooey goodness!

Nutrition Info (per serving): Calories: 350 | Fat: 15g | Carbs: 50g | Protein: 6g

PEANUT BUTTER AND JELLY ROLL-UP

Prep: 5 mins | Cook: 0 mins | Serves: 1
Cooking Function: None
Ingredients:
UK: 1 large tortilla, 30g peanut butter, 30g strawberry jam, sliced banana (optional)
US: 1 large tortilla, 1 oz peanut butter, 1 oz strawberry jam, sliced banana (optional)
Instructions:
1. Spread peanut butter evenly across the tortilla.
2. Add a layer of strawberry jam over the peanut butter.
3. If using, top with sliced banana.
4. Roll the tortilla tightly and slice into pinwheels.
5. Serve as a quick, delicious snack!

Nutrition Info (per serving): Calories: 350 | Fat: 16g | Carbs: 43g | Protein: 10g

BLUEBERRY CHEESECAKE WRAP

Prep: 10 mins | Cook: 0 mins | Serves: 2
Cooking Function: None
Ingredients:
UK: 2 large tortillas, 100g cream cheese, 30g icing sugar, 100g blueberries, 10g digestive biscuit crumbs
US: 2 large tortillas, 3.5 oz cream cheese, 1 oz icing sugar, 3.5 oz blueberries, 0.4 oz digestive biscuit crumbs
Instructions:
1. In a bowl, mix cream cheese and icing sugar until smooth.
2. Spread the cream cheese mixture on each tortilla.
3. Top with blueberries and sprinkle with biscuit crumbs.
4. Roll tightly and slice in half. Serve chilled for a creamy treat!

Nutrition Info (per serving): Calories: 300 | Fat: 15g | Carbs: 32g | Protein: 6g

CINNAMON SUGAR CHURRO WRAP

Prep: 10 mins | **Cook:** 10 mins | **Serves:** 4

Cooking Function: Air Fry

Ingredients:

UK: 4 large flour tortillas, 30g butter (melted), 50g sugar, 1 teaspoon cinnamon

US: 4 large flour tortillas, 1 oz butter, 1.8 oz sugar, 1 teaspoon cinnamon

Instructions:

1. Preheat your air fryer to 180°C (356°F).
2. Brush melted butter over each tortilla.
3. In a bowl, mix sugar and cinnamon, then sprinkle over the tortillas.
4. Roll each tortilla tightly and place it in the air fryer.
5. Cook for 8-10 minutes until crispy and golden.
6. Allow to cool slightly before slicing and serving.

Nutrition Info (per serving): Calories: 250 | Fat: 10g | Carbs: 37g | Protein: 4g

LEMON MERINGUE WRAP

Prep: 15 mins | **Cook:** 5 mins | **Serves:** 2

Cooking Function: Air Fry

Ingredients:

UK: 2 large tortillas, 100g lemon curd, 2 egg whites, 30g sugar, lemon zest (for garnish)

US: 2 large tortillas, 3.5 oz lemon curd, 1 oz egg whites, 1 oz sugar, lemon zest

Instructions:

1. Preheat your air fryer to 200°C (392°F).
2. Spread lemon curd on each tortilla.
3. In a bowl, whisk egg whites until soft peaks form. Gradually add sugar and continue whisking until glossy.
4. Spread the meringue over the lemon curd.
5. Place in the air fryer and cook for 5 minutes until the meringue is golden.
6. Garnish with lemon zest before serving!

Nutrition Info (per serving): Calories: 220 | Fat: 5g | Carbs: 28g | Protein: 4g

CHOCOLATE AND MARSHMALLOW WRAP

Prep: 5 mins | **Cook:** 5 mins | **Serves:** 2
Cooking Function: Air Fry
Ingredients:
UK: 2 large tortillas, 60g dark chocolate (chopped), 50g mini marshmallows
US: 2 large tortillas, 2 oz dark chocolate, 1.8 oz mini marshmallows
Instructions:
1. Preheat your air fryer to 180°C (356°F).
2. Place chopped chocolate and marshmallows in the centre of each tortilla.
3. Roll the tortillas tightly and place them in the air fryer.
4. Cook for 5 minutes until the chocolate is melted and the tortillas are golden.
5. Slice and serve warm for a decadent dessert!

Nutrition Info (per serving): Calories: 320 | Fat: 15g | Carbs: 45g | Protein: 4g

PEACHES AND CREAM WRAP

Prep: 10 mins | **Cook:** 0 mins | **Serves:** 2
Cooking Function: None
Ingredients:
UK: 2 large tortillas, 200g peaches (sliced), 60ml double cream (whipped), 20g honey
US: 2 large tortillas, 7 oz peaches, 2 oz double cream, 0.7 oz honey
Instructions:
1. Spread whipped double cream on each tortilla.
2. Layer with sliced peaches and drizzle with honey.
3. Roll tightly and cut into pinwheels.
4. Serve immediately for a refreshing dessert!

Nutrition Info (per serving): Calories: 280 | Fat: 9g | Carbs: 42g | Protein: 3g

BANOFFEE PIE WRAP

Prep: 10 mins | **Cook:** 5 mins | **Serves:** 2
Cooking Function: Air Fry
Ingredients:
UK: 2 large tortillas, 100g toffee sauce, 2 bananas (sliced), 60ml double cream (whipped)
US: 2 large tortillas, 3.5 oz toffee sauce, 2 bananas, 2 oz double cream

Instructions:
1. Spread toffee sauce on each tortilla.
2. Add banana slices evenly.
3. Roll up tightly and place in the air fryer.
4. Cook for 5 minutes until golden and warm.
5. Drizzle with whipped cream before serving!

Nutrition Info (per serving): Calories: 400 | Fat: 18g | Carbs: 58g | Protein: 5g

BERRY YOGURT PARFAIT WRAP

Prep: 10 mins | Cook: 0 mins | Serves: 2
Cooking Function: None
Ingredients:
UK: 2 large tortillas, 200g Greek yogurt, 100g mixed berries, 30g granola
US: 2 large tortillas, 7 oz Greek yogurt, 3.5 oz mixed berries, 1 oz granola

Instructions:
1. Spread Greek yoghurt evenly on each tortilla.
2. Top with mixed berries and sprinkle with granola.
3. Roll tightly and slice in half. Serve chilled for a refreshing treat!

Nutrition Info (per serving): Calories: 250 | Fat: 6g | Carbs: 37g | Protein: 10g

TROPICAL FRUIT SALAD WRAP

Prep: 10 mins | Cook: 0 mins | Serves: 2
Cooking Function: None
Ingredients:
UK: 2 large tortillas, 100g pineapple (diced), 100g mango (diced), 50g kiwi (sliced), 30g shredded coconut
US: 2 large tortillas, 3.5 oz pineapple, 3.5 oz mango, 1.8 oz kiwi, 1 oz shredded coconut

Instructions:
1. Mix diced pineapple, mango, and kiwi in a bowl.
2. Spread the fruit mixture evenly on each tortilla.
3. Sprinkle with shredded coconut.
4. Roll tightly and cut into pinwheels. Serve fresh for a fruity delight!

Nutrition Info (per serving): Calories: 200 | Fat: 3g | Carbs: 40g | Protein: 2g

CHAPTER 9: SAUCES, SPREADS, AND DIPS

CLASSIC HUMMUS

Prep: 10 mins | **Cook:** 0 mins | **Serves:** 4

Cooking Function: None

Ingredients:

UK: 400g canned chickpeas (drained and rinsed), 60ml tahini, 30ml olive oil, 30ml lemon juice, 1 garlic clove (minced), ½ teaspoon ground cumin, salt to taste, water (as needed)

US: 14 oz canned chickpeas, 2 oz tahini, 1 oz olive oil, 1 oz lemon juice, 1 garlic clove, ½ teaspoon ground cumin, salt to taste, water (as needed)

Instructions:

1. In a food processor, combine chickpeas, tahini, olive oil, lemon juice, minced garlic, cumin, and salt.
2. Blend until smooth, adding water as needed to achieve your desired consistency.
3. Taste and adjust seasoning if necessary.
4. Serve the Classic Hummus drizzled with olive oil, and enjoy with your favourite wraps or veggies!

Nutrition Info (per serving): Calories: 220 | Fat: 10g | Carbs: 27g | Protein: 7g

TZATZIKI SAUCE

Prep: 10 mins | **Cook:** 0 mins | **Serves:** 4

Cooking Function: None

Ingredients:

UK: 200g Greek yoghurt, 1 cucumber (grated and drained), 1 garlic clove (minced), 30ml olive oil, 15ml lemon juice, salt and pepper to taste, chopped fresh dill (for garnish)

US: 7 oz Greek yoghurt, 1 cucumber, 1 garlic clove, 1 oz olive oil, ½ oz lemon juice, salt and pepper to taste, fresh dill

Instructions:

1. In a bowl, combine Greek yoghurt, grated cucumber, minced garlic, olive oil, lemon juice, salt, and pepper.
2. Mix well until all ingredients are fully combined.
3. Garnish with chopped dill.
4. Serve your Tzatziki Sauce as a refreshing dip for wraps or grilled meats!

Nutrition Info (per serving): Calories: 150 | Fat: 9g | Carbs: 6g | Protein: 8g

GUACAMOLE

Prep: 10 mins | Cook: 0 mins | Serves: 4
Cooking Function: None
Ingredients:

UK: 2 ripe avocados, 1 lime (juiced), 1 small onion (finely chopped), 1 tomato (diced), 1 garlic clove (minced), salt to taste, chopped fresh coriander (for garnish)

US: 2 ripe avocados, 1 lime, 1 small onion, 1 tomato, 1 garlic clove, salt to taste, fresh coriander

Instructions:

1. In a bowl, mash the avocados with a fork until smooth.
2. Stir in lime juice, onion, tomato, minced garlic, and salt.
3. Mix well until combined.
4. Garnish with fresh coriander.
5. Enjoy your Guacamole with wraps, chips, or veggies for a delicious twist!

Nutrition Info (per serving): Calories: 200 | Fat: 15g | Carbs: 12g | Protein: 3g

SALSA FRESCA

Prep: 10 mins | Cook: 0 mins | Serves: 4
Cooking Function: None
Ingredients:

UK: 4 ripe tomatoes (diced), 1 small onion (finely chopped), 1 jalapeño (seeded and diced), 15ml lime juice, salt and pepper to taste, chopped fresh coriander (for garnish)

US: 4 ripe tomatoes, 1 small onion, 1 jalapeño, ½ oz lime juice, salt and pepper to taste, fresh coriander

Instructions:

1. In a bowl, combine diced tomatoes, onion, jalapeño, lime juice, salt, and pepper.
2. Mix well to ensure everything is evenly coated.
3. Garnish with fresh coriander.
4. Serve your Salsa Fresca with wraps, tacos, or as a fresh topping for grilled meats!

Nutrition Info (per serving): Calories: 50 | Fat: 0g | Carbs: 12g | Protein: 2g

GARLIC AIOLI

Prep: 10 mins | **Cook:** 0 mins | **Serves:** 4
Cooking Function: None
Ingredients:
UK: 100g mayonnaise, 2 garlic cloves (minced), 15ml lemon juice, salt and pepper to taste, chopped fresh parsley (for garnish)
US: 3.5 oz mayonnaise, 2 garlic cloves, ½ oz lemon juice, salt and pepper to taste, fresh parsley
Instructions:
1. In a bowl, mix mayonnaise, minced garlic, lemon juice, salt, and pepper until well combined.
2. Taste and adjust seasoning as needed.
3. Garnish with fresh parsley.
4. Serve your Garlic Aioli as a creamy dip for wraps or a tasty spread for sandwiches!

Nutrition Info (per serving): Calories: 100 | Fat: 10g | Carbs: 2g | Protein: 1g

TAHINI SAUCE

Prep: 5 mins | **Cook:** 0 mins | **Serves:** 4
Cooking Function: None
Ingredients:
UK: 60g tahini, 30ml lemon juice, 30ml water, 1 garlic clove (minced), salt to taste, chopped fresh parsley (for garnish)
US: 2 oz tahini, 1 oz lemon juice, 1 oz water, 1 garlic clove, salt to taste, fresh parsley
Instructions:
1. In a bowl, whisk together tahini, lemon juice, water, minced garlic, and salt until smooth.
2. Adjust the consistency with more water if needed.
3. Garnish with fresh parsley.
4. Use your Tahini Sauce as a drizzle over wraps or a dip for fresh veggies!

Nutrition Info (per serving): Calories: 140 | Fat: 10g | Carbs: 9g | Protein: 4g

PESTO

Prep: 10 mins | **Cook:** 0 mins | **Serves:** 4
Cooking Function: None
Ingredients:
UK: 50g fresh basil leaves, 30g pine nuts, 30g Parmesan cheese (grated), 60ml olive oil, 1 garlic clove (minced), salt to taste
US: 1.7 oz fresh basil leaves, 1 oz pine nuts, 1 oz Parmesan cheese, 2 oz olive oil, 1 garlic clove, salt to taste
Instructions:
1. In a food processor, combine basil leaves, pine nuts, Parmesan cheese, olive oil, minced garlic, and salt.
2. Blend until smooth, scraping down the sides as necessary.
3. Serve your Pesto as a spread for wraps or a sauce for pasta!

Nutrition Info (per serving): Calories: 200 | Fat: 18g | Carbs: 4g | Protein: 6g

CHIPOTLE MAYO

Prep: 5 mins | **Cook:** 0 mins | **Serves:** 4
Cooking Function: None
Ingredients:
UK: 100g mayonnaise, 15g chipotle sauce, 10ml lime juice, salt to taste
US: 3.5 oz mayonnaise, 0.5 oz chipotle sauce, 0.5 oz lime juice, salt to taste
Instructions:
1. In a bowl, mix mayonnaise, chipotle sauce, lime juice, and salt until well blended.
2. Adjust seasoning to taste.
3. Use your Chipotle Mayo as a spicy dip for wraps or a zesty spread for sandwiches!

Nutrition Info (per serving): Calories: 120 | Fat: 12g | Carbs: 2g | Protein: 1g

MANGO CHUTNEY

Prep: 10 mins | **Cook:** 20 mins | **Serves:** 4
Cooking Function: None
Ingredients:

UK: 400g ripe mango (diced), 50g sugar, 30ml apple cider vinegar, 1 garlic clove (minced), 1 teaspoon grated ginger, salt to taste

US: 14 oz ripe mango, 1.75 oz sugar, 1 oz apple cider vinegar, 1 garlic clove, 1 teaspoon grated ginger, salt to taste

Instructions:

1. In a saucepan, combine diced mango, sugar, apple cider vinegar, minced garlic, grated ginger, and salt.
2. Cook over medium heat for 20 minutes, stirring occasionally until thickened.
3. Let cool before serving.
4. Enjoy your Mango Chutney as a sweet and tangy addition to wraps or grilled meats!

Nutrition Info (per serving): Calories: 150 | Fat: 0g | Carbs: 38g | Protein: 1g

BBQ SAUCE

Prep: 5 mins | **Cook:** 15 mins | **Serves:** 4
Cooking Function: None
Ingredients:

UK: 200g ketchup, 50g brown sugar, 30ml apple cider vinegar, 15ml Worcestershire sauce, 1 teaspoon smoked paprika, salt and pepper to taste

US: 7 oz ketchup, 1.75 oz brown sugar, 1 oz apple cider vinegar, 0.5 oz Worcestershire sauce, 1 teaspoon smoked paprika, salt and pepper to taste

Instructions:

1. In a saucepan, mix ketchup, brown sugar, apple cider vinegar, Worcestershire sauce, smoked paprika, salt, and pepper.
2. Cook over medium heat for 15 minutes, stirring until heated through.
3. Let cool slightly before serving.
4. Use your BBQ Sauce as a perfect complement to wraps or grilled dishes!

Nutrition Info (per serving): Calories: 80 | Fat: 0g | Carbs: 20g | Protein: 1g

SWEET CHILLI SAUCE

Prep: 5 mins | **Cook:** 10 mins | **Serves:** 4
Cooking Function: None
Ingredients:

UK: 100g sugar, 60ml rice vinegar, 30ml water, 30g red chillies (chopped), 1 garlic clove (minced), salt to taste

US: 3.5 oz sugar, 2 oz rice vinegar, 1 oz water, 1 oz red chillies, 1 garlic clove, salt to taste

Instructions:

1. In a saucepan, combine sugar, rice vinegar, water, chopped chillies, minced garlic, and salt.
2. Bring to a boil, then reduce heat and simmer for 10 minutes.
3. Allow to cool before serving.
4. Enjoy your Sweet Chilli Sauce as a delightful dip for wraps or spring rolls!

Nutrition Info (per serving): Calories: 100 | Fat: 0g | Carbs: 25g | Protein: 0g

HERBY YOGURT DIP

Prep: 10 mins | **Cook:** 0 mins | **Serves:** 4

Cooking Function: None

Ingredients:

UK: 200g Greek yoghurt, 30ml olive oil, 1 garlic clove (minced), 15ml lemon juice, salt and pepper to taste, chopped fresh herbs (e.g., parsley, chives)

US: 7 oz Greek yoghurt, 1 oz olive oil, 1 garlic clove, ½ oz lemon juice, salt and pepper to taste, fresh herbs

Instructions:

1. In a bowl, mix Greek yoghurt, olive oil, minced garlic, lemon juice, salt, and pepper until well combined.
2. Stir in chopped fresh herbs.
3. Serve your Herby Yogurt Dip as a fresh accompaniment for wraps or veggies!

Nutrition Info (per serving): Calories: 120 | Fat: 8g | Carbs: 4g | Protein: 6g

BABA GANOUSH

Prep: 10 mins | **Cook:** 30 mins | **Serves:** 4

Cooking Function: Roast

Ingredients:

UK: 1 large aubergine (eggplant), 60ml tahini, 30ml lemon juice, 1 garlic clove (minced), 30ml olive oil, salt and pepper to taste, chopped fresh parsley (for garnish)

US: 1 large eggplant, 2 oz tahini, 1 oz lemon juice, 1 garlic clove, 1 oz olive oil, salt and pepper to taste, fresh parsley

Instructions:

1. Preheat the oven to 200°C (400°F).
2. Prick the aubergine with a fork and roast it on a baking tray for about 30 minutes, or until the skin is charred and the flesh is soft.
3. Allow the aubergine to cool, then scoop the flesh into a bowl.
4. Add tahini, lemon juice, minced garlic, olive oil, salt, and pepper.
5. Blend until smooth.
6. Garnish with fresh parsley before serving.
7. Enjoy your Baba Ganoush as a smoky dip with wraps or pita!

Nutrition Info (per serving): Calories: 150 | Fat: 10g | Carbs: 15g | Protein: 3g

CHAPTER 10: SIDE DISHES AND ACCOMPANIMENTS

CRISPY SWEET POTATO FRIES

Prep: 10 mins | Cook: 20 mins | Serves: 4

Cooking Function: Air Fry

Ingredients:

UK: 600g sweet potatoes (peeled and cut into fries), 30ml olive oil, 1 teaspoon paprika, salt and pepper to taste

US: 21 oz sweet potatoes, 1 oz olive oil, 1 teaspoon paprika, salt and pepper to taste

Instructions:

1. Preheat the air fryer to 200°C (400°F).
2. In a large bowl, toss the sweet potato fries with olive oil, paprika, salt, and pepper until evenly coated.
3. Place the fries in the air fryer basket in a single layer.
4. Cook for 15-20 minutes, shaking the basket halfway through, until they are crispy and golden.
5. Serve the crispy sweet potato fries hot, perfect for dipping into your favourite sauces!

Nutrition Info (per serving): Calories: 180 | Fat: 7g | Carbs: 30g | Protein: 2g

GREEK SALAD

Prep: 10 mins | Cook: 0 mins | Serves: 4

Cooking Function: None

Ingredients:

UK: 200g cherry tomatoes (halved), 150g cucumber (diced), 100g red onion (sliced), 150g feta cheese (cubed), 30ml olive oil, 15ml red wine vinegar, salt, pepper, chopped fresh parsley (for garnish)

US: 7 oz cherry tomatoes, 5 oz cucumber, 3.5 oz red onion, 5 oz feta cheese, 1 oz olive oil, 0.5 oz red wine vinegar, salt, pepper, fresh parsley

Instructions:

1. In a large bowl, combine cherry tomatoes, cucumber, red onion, and feta cheese.
2. Drizzle with olive oil and red wine vinegar, then season with salt and pepper.
3. Gently toss everything together until well-mixed.
4. Garnish with fresh parsley before serving.
5. Enjoy your Greek salad chilled as a refreshing side for wraps!

Nutrition Info (per serving): Calories: 150 | Fat: 12g | Carbs: 8g | Protein: 4g

COLESLAW

Prep: 15 mins | **Cook:** 0 mins | **Serves:** 4
Cooking Function: None
Ingredients:

UK: 300g white cabbage (shredded), 150g carrots (grated), 100g mayonnaise, 15ml apple cider vinegar, 1 teaspoon sugar, salt, and pepper to taste

US: 10.5 oz white cabbage, 5.5 oz carrots, 3.5 oz mayonnaise, 0.5 oz apple cider vinegar, 1 teaspoon sugar, salt, and pepper to taste

Instructions:

1. In a large bowl, mix the shredded cabbage and grated carrots.
2. In a separate bowl, whisk together mayonnaise, apple cider vinegar, sugar, salt, and pepper.
3. Pour the dressing over the cabbage and carrot mixture, and toss until everything is coated.
4. Chill in the fridge for at least 30 minutes before serving.
5. Serve your coleslaw cold as a crunchy accompaniment to wraps!

Nutrition Info (per serving): Calories: 220 | Fat: 18g | Carbs: 12g | Protein: 2g

TABBOULEH

Prep: 15 mins | **Cook:** 0 mins | **Serves:** 4
Cooking Function: None
Ingredients:

UK: 100g bulgur wheat, 250ml water, 150g tomatoes (diced), 50g cucumber (diced), 30g fresh parsley (chopped), 15ml lemon juice, 30ml olive oil, salt and pepper to taste

US: 3.5 oz bulgur wheat, 8.5 oz water, 5.5 oz tomatoes, 1.75 oz cucumber, 1 oz fresh parsley, 0.5 oz lemon juice, 1 oz olive oil, salt, and pepper to taste

Instructions:

1. Rinse the bulgur wheat under cold water, then place it in a bowl and pour boiling water over it. Cover and let it sit for about 15 minutes, or until the water is absorbed.
2. Fluff the bulgur with a fork and let it cool.
3. In a large bowl, combine the cooled bulgur, tomatoes, cucumber, parsley, lemon juice, olive oil, salt, and pepper.
4. Toss well and adjust the seasoning if needed.
5. Serve your tabbouleh fresh as a vibrant side dish for wraps!

Nutrition Info (per serving): Calories: 140 | Fat: 7g | Carbs: 17g | Protein: 4g

POTATO WEDGES

Prep: 10 mins | **Cook:** 30 mins | **Serves:** 4
Cooking Function: Air Fry
Ingredients:
UK: 800g potatoes (cut into wedges), 30ml olive oil, 1 teaspoon garlic powder, 1 teaspoon paprika, salt, and pepper to taste
US: 28 oz potatoes, 1 oz olive oil, 1 teaspoon garlic powder, 1 teaspoon paprika, salt, and pepper to taste
Instructions:
1. Preheat the air fryer to 200°C (400°F).
2. In a bowl, toss the potato wedges with olive oil, garlic powder, paprika, salt, and pepper until evenly coated.
3. Place the wedges in the air fryer basket in a single layer.
4. Cook for 25-30 minutes, shaking the basket halfway through, until golden and crispy.
5. Serve the potato wedges hot as a delightful side for wraps!
Nutrition Info (per serving): Calories: 200 | Fat: 9g | Carbs: 33g | Protein: 4g

CORN ON THE COB

Prep: 5 mins | **Cook:** 15 mins | **Serves:** 4
Cooking Function: Steam
Ingredients:
UK: 4 corn cobs, 30g butter, salt, pepper, chopped fresh herbs (for garnish)
US: 4 corn cobs, 1 oz butter, salt, pepper, fresh herbs
Instructions:
1. Steam the corn cobs for about 10-15 minutes until tender.
2. Remove from the steamer and spread butter over each cob.
3. Season with salt and pepper, and garnish with fresh herbs.
4. Serve your corn on the cob warm as a sweet side for wraps!
Nutrition Info (per serving): Calories: 130 | Fat: 6g | Carbs: 20g | Protein: 4g

GARLIC GREEN BEANS

Prep: 5 mins | **Cook:** 10 mins | **Serves:** 4
Cooking Function: Steam
Ingredients:
UK: 400g green beans (trimmed), 30g butter, 2 garlic cloves (minced), salt, and pepper to taste
US: 14 oz green beans, 1 oz butter, 2 garlic cloves, salt, and pepper to taste
Instructions:
1. Steam the green beans for about 5-7 minutes until tender but still crisp.
2. In a frying pan, melt the butter and sauté the minced garlic for 1-2 minutes until fragrant.
3. Add the steamed green beans to the pan, season with salt and pepper, and toss to coat.
4. Serve your garlic green beans hot as a zesty side for wraps!

Nutrition Info (per serving): Calories: 100 | Fat: 7g | Carbs: 8g | Protein: 2g

ROASTED MEDITERRANEAN VEGETABLES

Prep: 15 mins | **Cook:** 25 mins | **Serves:** 4
Cooking Function: Roast
Ingredients:
UK: 200g bell peppers (sliced), 200g courgettes (sliced), 200g red onion (sliced), 30ml olive oil, 1 teaspoon dried oregano, salt, and pepper to taste
US: 7 oz bell peppers, 7 oz zucchini, 7 oz red onion, 1 oz olive oil, 1 teaspoon dried oregano, salt, and pepper to taste
Instructions:
1. Preheat the oven to 200°C (400°F).
2. In a large bowl, toss the bell peppers, courgettes, and red onion with olive oil, oregano, salt, and pepper until well coated.
3. Spread the vegetables on a baking tray in a single layer.
4. Roast for 20-25 minutes, until tender and slightly charred.
5. Serve your roasted Mediterranean vegetables warm as a tasty side for wraps!

Nutrition Info (per serving): Calories: 120 | Fat: 8g | Carbs: 14g | Protein: 2g

QUINOA SALAD

Prep: 10 mins | **Cook:** 15 mins | **Serves:** 4
Cooking Function: Boil
Ingredients:
UK: 200g quinoa, 500ml water, 150g cherry tomatoes (halved), 100g cucumber (diced), 30ml olive oil, 15ml lemon juice, salt, and pepper to taste
US: 7 oz quinoa, 17 oz water, 5.5 oz cherry tomatoes, 3.5 oz cucumber, 1 oz olive oil, 0.5 oz lemon juice, salt, and pepper to taste
Instructions:
1. Rinse the quinoa under cold water.
2. In a pot, bring water to a boil and add the quinoa. Reduce to a simmer and cook for 15 minutes, until the water is absorbed.
3. Fluff the quinoa with a fork and let it cool.
4. In a bowl, combine the cooled quinoa, cherry tomatoes, cucumber, olive oil, lemon juice, salt, and pepper.
5. Serve your quinoa salad chilled as a nutritious side for wraps!

Nutrition Info (per serving): Calories: 160 | Fat: 7g | Carbs: 23g | Protein: 5g

PICKLED ONIONS

Prep: 10 mins | **Cook:** 0 mins | **Serves:** 4
Cooking Function: None
Ingredients:
UK: 1 red onion (thinly sliced), 125ml apple cider vinegar, 125ml water, 1 tablespoon sugar, salt to taste
US: 1 red onion, 4.5 oz apple cider vinegar, 4.5 oz water, 1 tablespoon sugar, salt to taste
Instructions:
1. In a bowl, whisk together apple cider vinegar, water, sugar, and salt until the sugar dissolves.
2. Add the sliced red onion to the mixture and ensure they're submerged.
3. Let them sit for at least 30 minutes before serving.
4. Serve your pickled onions as a tangy topping for wraps!

Nutrition Info (per serving): Calories: 25 | Fat: 0g | Carbs: 6g | Protein: 0g

CAJUN RICE

Prep: 10 mins | **Cook:** 20 mins | **Serves:** 4
Cooking Function: Cook
Ingredients:

UK: 200g long-grain rice, 400ml vegetable broth, 1 teaspoon Cajun seasoning, 100g bell peppers (diced), 100g onion (diced), 30ml olive oil, salt to taste

US: 7 oz long-grain rice, 14 oz vegetable broth, 1 teaspoon Cajun seasoning, 3.5 oz bell peppers, 3.5 oz onion, 1 oz olive oil, salt to taste

Instructions:

1. In a pot, heat olive oil over medium heat and sauté the diced onion and bell peppers until soft.
2. Add the rice and Cajun seasoning, stirring for 1-2 minutes.
3. Pour in the vegetable broth and bring to a boil.
4. Reduce heat, cover, and simmer for 15-20 minutes until the rice is cooked.
5. Serve your Cajun rice warm as a spicy side for wraps!

Nutrition Info (per serving): Calories: 210 | Fat: 5g | Carbs: 38g | Protein: 4g

CUCUMBER AND MINT RAITA

Prep: 10 mins | **Cook:** 0 mins | **Serves:** 4
Cooking Function: None
Ingredients:

UK: 200g natural yoghurt, 100g cucumber (grated), 1 tablespoon fresh mint (chopped), 15ml lemon juice, salt to taste

US: 7 oz natural yoghurt, 3.5 oz cucumber, 1 tablespoon fresh mint, 0.5 oz lemon juice, salt to taste

Instructions:

1. In a bowl, mix the yoghurt, grated cucumber, mint, lemon juice, and salt.
2. Stir well until combined.
3. Chill in the fridge for at least 30 minutes before serving.
4. Serve your cucumber and mint raita as a cooling dip for wraps!

Nutrition Info (per serving): Calories: 70 | Fat: 3g | Carbs: 6g | Protein: 5g

SPICY KIMCHI

Prep: 15 mins | **Cook:** 0 mins | **Serves:** 4

Cooking Function: None

Ingredients:

UK: 300g napa cabbage (chopped), 30g salt, 100g radishes (sliced), 2 green onions (chopped), 30ml fish sauce, 1 tablespoon Korean red pepper flakes (gochugaru), 15ml sugar, 2 garlic cloves (minced), 1 teaspoon grated ginger

US: 10.5 oz napa cabbage, 1 oz salt, 3.5 oz radishes, 2 green onions, 1 oz fish sauce, 1 tablespoon Korean red pepper flakes, 0.5 oz sugar, 2 garlic cloves, 1 teaspoon grated ginger

Instructions:

1. mix the chopped napa cabbage and salt in a large bowl, allowing it to wilt for about 2 hours.
2. Rinse the cabbage under cold water and drain well.
3. combine radishes, green onions, fish sauce, gochugaru, sugar, garlic, and ginger in another bowl.
4. Add the cabbage to the mixture and mix until evenly coated.
5. Pack the kimchi into a clean jar and let it ferment at room temperature for 2-3 days before refrigerating.
6. Serve your spicy kimchi as a tangy side for wraps!

Nutrition Info (per serving): Calories: 40 | Fat: 0g | Carbs: 8g | Protein: 1g

MEASUREMENT CONVERSIONS

Precise measurements can make all the difference when you're whipping up wraps. Here's a handy conversion chart to help you navigate between different measurement systems:

Volume		
Metric	Imperial	US Cups
5 ml	1 teaspoon	1 teaspoon
15 ml	1 tablespoon	1 tablespoon
60 ml	2 fl oz	1/4 cup
125 ml	4 fl oz	1/2 cup
250 ml	8 fl oz	1 cup
500 ml	16 fl oz (1 pint)	2 cups
1 litre	32 fl oz (1 quart)	4 cups

Weight	
Metric	Imperial
15 g	1/2 oz
30 g	1 oz
100 g	3.5 oz
225 g	8 oz (1/2 lb)
450 g	16 oz (1 lb)
1 kg	2.2 lbs

Temperature		
Celsius	Fahrenheit	Gas Mark
150°C	300°F	2
180°C	350°F	4
190°C	375°F	5
200°C	400°F	6
220°C	425°F	7
230°C	450°F	8

Remember, in baking, it's always best to use the measurement system specified in the recipe for the most accurate results.

MEAL PLAN TIMETABLE ACCORDING TO NUTRITION

This 60-day meal plan is designed to provide a balanced, nutritious diet using a variety of wraps. It's structured to ensure you're getting a good mix of proteins, carbohydrates, healthy fats, and plenty of fruits and vegetables.

Please note: This is a general guide. Always consult with a healthcare professional or registered dietitian before making significant changes to your diet, especially if you have any health conditions or dietary restrictions.

WEEK 1 Mediterranean Week

DAYS	BREAKFAST	LUNCH	Appetizer	DINNER
MONDAY	Greek Yogurt and Berry Breakfast Wrap	Greek Salad Wrap	Classic Hummus with Veggie Crudité Wraps	Lamb Kofta Wrap with Tzatziki
TUESDAY	Peanut Butter and Banana Breakfast Roll	Prawn and Avocado Wrap	Baba Ganoush with Pita Strips	Spinach and Ricotta Cannelloni Wrap
WEDNESDAY	Scrambled Tofu Breakfast Wrap	Chicken Caesar Wrap	Tabbouleh	Greek Gyros Wrap
THURSDAY	Avocado Toast Wrap	Tuna Nicoise Salad Wrap	Tzatziki Sauce with Zucchini Chips	Vegetable Stir-Fry Lettuce Wraps
FRIDAY	Full English Breakfast Burrito	Turkey and Cranberry Wrap	Roasted Mediterranean Vegetables	Falafel and Hummus Wrap
SATURDAY	Bacon, Egg, and Cheese Wrap	Coronation Chicken Wrap	Garlic Aioli with Sweet Potato Fries	BBQ Pulled Pork Wrap
SUNDAY (SPECIAL DINNER)	Mushroom and Spinach Breakfast Quesadilla	Ploughman's Lunch Wrap	Pickled Onions and Tabbouleh	Moroccan Lamb Wrap

WEEK 2 Global Flavours

DAYS	BREAKFAST	LUNCH	Appetizer	DINNER
MONDAY	Nutella and Strawberry Crepe Wrap	Middle Eastern Shawarma Wrap	Salsa Fresca with Tortilla Chips	Japanese Teriyaki Chicken Wrap
TUESDAY	Tofu Scramble Breakfast Wrap	Pesto Chicken and Mozzarella Wrap	Spicy Kimchi	Mexican Street Corn Wrap
WEDNESDAY	Ham and Cheese Breakfast Wrap	Vegan 'Chicken' Caesar Wrap	Guacamole with Vegetable Spring Rolls	Thai Green Curry Wrap
THURSDAY	Cinnamon Roll Bites	Greek Gyros Wrap	Classic Hummus	Italian Caprese Wrap
FRIDAY	Apple and Cinnamon Breakfast Burrito	Russian Beef Stroganoff Wrap	Garlic Green Beans	American Philly Cheesesteak Wrap
SATURDAY	Blueberry Cheesecake Wrap	Jamaican Jerk Chicken Wrap	Mango Chutney with Mini Pinwheels	Sausage and Mash Wrap
SUNDAY (SPECIAL DINNER)	Breakfast Pizza Squares	Club Sandwich Wrap	Egg and Watercress Finger Wraps	Indian Butter Chicken Wrap

WEEK 3 Healthy and Light

DAYS	BREAKFAST	LUNCH	Appetizer	DINNER
MONDAY	Sweet Potato Toast Two Ways	Turkey and Hummus Pinwheels	Cucumber and Mint Raita	Grilled Prawn and Mango Wrap
TUESDAY	Greek Yogurt and Berry Breakfast Wrap	Quinoa and Roasted Vegetable Wrap	Roasted Mediterranean Vegetables	Lentil and Sweet Potato Wrap
WEDNESDAY	Apple-Cinnamon Oatmeal Cups	Egg Mayonnaise and Cress Wrap	Herby Yogurt Dip with Zucchini Chips	Tofu and Vegetable Spring Rolls
THURSDAY	Avocado Toast Wrap	Tuna Salad Wrap	Garlic Green Beans	Cauliflower Rice and Black Bean Burrito
FRIDAY	Scrambled Tofu Breakfast Wrap	Greek Salad Wrap	Classic Hummus with Cucumber Sticks	Teriyaki Tofu Wrap
SATURDAY	Ham and Cheese Breakfast Wrap	Prawn and Avocado Wrap	Spicy Kimchi	Moroccan Lamb Wrap
SUNDAY (SPECIAL DINNER)	Banana and Nutella Crepe Wrap	Roast Beef and Horseradish Wrap	Pickled Onions	Fish and Chips Wrap

WEEK 4 Hearty Classics Week

DAYS	BREAKFAST	LUNCH	Appetizer	DINNER
MONDAY	Full English Breakfast Burrito	BLT Wrap	Garlic Aioli with Potato Wedges	Spicy Beef and Bean Burrito
TUESDAY	Peanut Butter and Jelly Roll-Up	Coronation Chicken Wrap	Tabbouleh	BBQ Pulled Pork Wrap
WEDNESDAY	Scrambled Tofu Breakfast Wrap	Roast Beef and Horseradish Wrap	Roasted Mediterranean Vegetables	Lamb Kofta Wrap with Tzatziki
THURSDAY	Bacon, Egg, and Cheese Wrap	Chicken Caesar Wrap	Sweet Chilli Sauce with Spring Rolls	Chicken Tikka Masala Wrap
FRIDAY	Mushroom and Spinach Quesadilla	Tuna Salad Wrap	Salsa Fresca with Tortilla Chips	Sausage and Mash Wrap
SATURDAY	Granola Clusters with Yogurt Wrap	Turkey and Cranberry Wrap	Pickled Onions with Antipasti Skewers	Vegetarian Chilli Wrap
SUNDAY (SPECIAL DINNER)	French Toast Sticks	Egg and Watercress Finger Wraps	Garlic Green Beans	Fajita-Style Steak Wrap

WEEK 5 Plant-Based Power

DAYS	BREAKFAST	LUNCH	Appetizer	DINNER
MONDAY	Vegan 'Egg' Mayo Wrap	Chickpea 'Tuna' Salad Wrap	Beetroot Hummus with Veggie Sticks	Falafel and Hummus Wrap
TUESDAY	Sweet Potato Toast Two Ways	Grilled Halloumi and Roasted Vegetable Wrap	Spicy Kimchi	Mushroom Shawarma Wrap
WEDNESDAY	Apple and Cinnamon Breakfast Burrito	Greek-Style Veggie Wrap	Baba Ganoush	Lentil and Spinach Curry Wrap
THURSDAY	Nutella and Strawberry Crepe Wrap	Caprese Wrap with Balsamic Glaze	Tzatziki Sauce with Zucchini Chips	Teriyaki Tofu Wrap
FRIDAY	Tofu Scramble Breakfast Wrap	Vegan 'Chicken' Caesar Wrap	Garlic Aioli with Sweet Potato Fries	Spicy Bean and Guacamole Burrito
SATURDAY	Breakfast Burrito Roll-Ups	Pesto and Sun-Dried Tomato Pinwheels	Roasted Butternut Squash with Sage	Vegan 'Fish' Finger Wrap
SUNDAY (SPECIAL DINNER)	Cinnamon Sugar Churro Wrap	Greek Salad Wrap	Pickled Onions	Moroccan Lamb Wrap

WEEK 6 Fusion Flavours

DAYS	BREAKFAST	LUNCH	Appetizer	DINNER
MONDAY	Blueberry Cheesecake Wrap	Vietnamese Banh Mi Wrap	Classic Hummus	Korean BBQ Beef Wrap
TUESDAY	Banana and Nutella Crepe Wrap	Middle Eastern Shawarma Wrap	Salsa Fresca with Tortilla Chips	Italian Caprese Wrap
WEDNESDAY	French Toast Sticks	Japanese Teriyaki Chicken Wrap	Herby Yogurt Dip with Crudité Veggies	American Philly Cheesesteak Wrap
THURSDAY	Greek Yogurt and Berry Wrap	Mexican Street Corn Wrap	Mango Chutney	Thai Green Curry Wrap
FRIDAY	Peanut Butter and Banana Roll	Russian Beef Stroganoff Wrap	Garlic Green Beans	Fish and Chips Wrap
SATURDAY	Scrambled Tofu Breakfast Wrap	BLT Wrap	Roasted Mediterranean Vegetables	BBQ Pulled Pork Wrap
SUNDAY (SPECIAL DINNER)	Apple Pie Wrap	Club Sandwich Wrap	Coleslaw	Lamb Kofta Wrap

WEEK 7 Healthy Comforts

DAYS	BREAKFAST	LUNCH	Appetizer	DINNER
MONDAY	Egg White and Spinach Wrap	Turkey and Hummus Pinwheels	Garlic Aioli with Sweet Potato Fries	Vegetable Stir-Fry Lettuce Wraps
TUESDAY	Tofu Scramble Breakfast Wrap	Tuna Nicoise Salad Wrap	Cucumber and Mint Raita	Grilled Prawn and Mango Wrap
WEDNESDAY	Sweet Potato Toast Two Ways	Vegan Rainbow Veggie Wrap Bites	Pickled Onions	Moroccan Lamb Wrap
THURSDAY	Nutella and Strawberry Crepe Wrap	Coronation Chicken Wrap	Salsa Fresca	Vegetarian Chilli Wrap
FRIDAY	Peanut Butter and Jelly Roll-Up	Prawn and Avocado Wrap	Spicy Kimchi	Teriyaki Tofu Wrap
SATURDAY	Avocado Toast Wrap	Egg Mayonnaise and Cress Wrap	Classic Hummus	Spicy Beef and Bean Burrito
SUNDAY (SPECIAL DINNER)	Breakfast Quesadilla	Ploughman's Lunch Wrap	Garlic Green Beans	Chicken Tikka Masala Wrap

WEEK 8 Party Wraps and Celebration Flavours

DAYS	BREAKFAST	LUNCH	Appetizer	DINNER
MONDAY	Banana and Nutella Crepe	Turkey and Hummus Pinwheels	Vegetable Crudité Hummus Wraps	BBQ Pulled Pork Wrap
TUESDAY	Greek Yogurt and Berry Breakfast Wrap	Prawn Cocktail Lettuce Cups	Spicy Kimchi	Korean BBQ Beef Wrap
WEDNESDAY	Peanut Butter and Banana Breakfast Roll	Ham and Cheese Wrap Straws	Herby Yogurt Dip with Zucchini Chips	American Philly Cheesesteak Wrap
THURSDAY	Mushroom and Spinach Quesadilla	Coronation Chicken Vol-au-Wrap	Mango Chutney	Moroccan Lamb Wrap
FRIDAY	Cinnamon Sugar Churro Wrap	Mini Wrap Pinwheels Platter	Classic Hummus with Pickled Onions	Fajita-Style Steak Wrap
SATURDAY	Avocado Toast Wrap	Egg and Watercress Finger Wraps	Roasted Mediterranean Vegetables	Fish and Chips Wrap
SUNDAY (SPECIAL DINNER)	Apple Pie Wrap	Club Sandwich Wrap	Garlic Green Beans	Crispy Duck Pancakes

DAYS 57–60: GRAND FINALE – PARTY FEAST WEEK
Use these last few days as a celebration of the best wraps!

Breakfast Ideas:
- French Toast Sticks
- Nutella and Strawberry Crepe Wrap
- Blueberry Cheesecake Wrap
- Peanut Butter and Jelly Roll-Up

Lunch Ideas:
- Pesto and Sun-Dried Tomato Pinwheels
- Greek Salad Wrap
- Ploughman's Lunch Wrap
- Vegan Rainbow Veggie Wrap Bites

Appetisers & Sides:
- Antipasti Wrap Skewers
- Potato Wedges with Garlic Aioli
- Vegetable Spring Rolls with Sweet Chilli Sauce
- Cucumber and Mint Raita

Dinner Ideas:
- Chicken Tikka Masala Wrap
- Lamb Kofta Wrap with Tzatziki
- Thai Green Curry Wrap
- Vegetarian Chilli Wrap

Special Desserts:
- S'mores Wrap
- Peaches and Cream Wrap
- Lemon Meringue Wrap
- Banoffee Pie Wrap

Summary and Meal Plan Benefits
This 60-day wrap plan brings variety, nutrition, and global flavours to your table, with a perfect balance between hearty meals, plant-based options, festive party wraps, and light snacks. It's designed to keep you engaged with new flavours daily, featuring:

Healthy breakfasts to kickstart your day.

Lunch box heroes are ideal for work or on-the-go meals.

Appetisers and sides to complement your dinners or parties.

Special Sunday dinners for a delightful end to each week.

Sweet treats to indulge in during the final days of the plan.

Enjoy every bite of this delicious culinary journey, and feel free to mix and match your favourite wraps to suit your lifestyle!

INGREDIENT SUBSTITUTIONS

Sometimes you might find yourself missing an ingredient or needing to cater to dietary restrictions. Here are some common substitutions that work well in wraps:

WRAPS

Original	Substitution
Flour tortilla	Whole wheat tortilla, corn tortilla, lettuce leaf, rice paper, nori sheet
Pita bread	Lavash, flatbread, tortilla
Bread	Any type of wrap

Proteins

Original	Substitution
Chicken	Turkey, tofu, tempeh, seitan, chickpeas
Beef	Lamb, pork, textured vegetable protein (TVP
Fish	Canned tuna or salmon, tofu, tempeh
Eggs	Scrambled tofu, chickpea 'egg' salad

Vegetables

Original	Substitution
Lettuce	Spinach, kale, cabbage, rocket
Tomatoes	Bell peppers, sundried tomatoes
Onions	Spring onions, leeks, shallots
Cucumber	Courgette, celery

Dairy

Original	Substitution
Cheese	Nutritional yeast, vegan cheese, avocado
Yoghurt	Coconut yoghurt, soy yoghurt, mashed avocado
Cream cheese	Hummus, nut-based cheese spread.

Sauces and Spreads	
Original	Substitution
Mayonnaise	Greek yoghurt, mashed avocado, hummus
Hummus	Baba ganoush, mashed beans, nut butter
Salsa	Chopped tomatoes and onions, chutney

Remember, these substitutions may change the flavour or texture of your wrap, but they can be a great way to accommodate dietary needs or preferences, or simply to try something new! Don't be afraid to experiment and find your favourite substitutions.

Printed in Great Britain
by Amazon